CW00394674

Earthbound

Paul Morley

PENGUIN BOOKS

PENGUIN BOOKS

Published by the Penguin Group
Penguin Books Ltd, 80 Strand, London WC2R 0RL, England
Penguin Group (USA) Inc., 375 Hudson Street, New York, New York 10014, USA
Penguin Group (Canada), 90 Eglinton Avenue East, Suite 700, Toronto, Ontario,
Canada M4P 2Y3 (a division of Pearson Penguin Canada Inc.)
Penguin Ireland, 25 St Stephen's Green, Dublin 2, Ireland (a division of Penguin Books Ltd)
Penguin Group (Australia), 707 Collins Street, Melbourne, Victoria 3008, Australia
(a division of Pearson Australia Group Pty Ltd)
Penguin Books India Pvt Ltd, 11 Community Centre, Panchsheel Park, New Delhi – 110 017, India
Penguin Group (NZ), 67 Apollo Drive, Rosedale, Auckland 0632, New Zealand
(a division of Pearson New Zealand Ltd)
Penguin Books (South Africa) (Pty) Ltd, Block D, Rosebank Office Park, 181 Jan Smuts Avenue,
Parktown North, Gauteng 2193, South Africa

Penguin Books Ltd, Registered Offices: 80 Strand, London WC2R 0RL, England

www.penguin.com

First published in Penguin Books 2013
001

Set in 11.75/15pt Baskerville MT Std
Typeset by Jouve (UK), Milton Keynes
Printed in England by Clays Ltd, St Ives plc

ISBN: 978-1-846-14645-9

www.greenpenguin.co.uk

Penguin Books is committed to a sustainable
future for our business, our readers and our planet.
This book is made from Forest Stewardship
Council™ certified paper.

ALWAYS LEARNING   **PEARSON**

I

I can't remember the exact first time I ever travelled on the Tube. Not because I first used it as a child and have forgotten the day it happened, the memory suffering next to other, more tenacious memories. I grew up in Stockport, six miles south of Manchester, and the first time I visited London, in search of music, and new experience, was when I was seventeen or eighteen. I know I used the Tube on those trips, but even that relatively late memory has not fared well compared to other memories of first working out London and its loaded, scattered ways.

There must have been a time when that was a real moment, the first time I did something never done before, and what a thing to do if you think about it. A first time that I entered a Tube station, bought a ticket, stood on an escalator, gliding deep under the ground, with a look on my face indicating slight concern about what might be down there. Would it be hot, cold, dark, stocked with latent dangers? Then I walked along a tiled enigmatic corridor past sudden turnings, barren corners, sly hiding places, battered metal doors stamped with no-nonsense no-entry signs towards a platform where I stood waiting for my first ever Underground train. It would roar into the station, shooting out of the tunnel, like it was blasting out of the dark, disordered past, with an exotic history all its own, believing in the illusion of continuity, before its doors opened, and it invited me in, for a few seconds of collective, collecting lit-up stillness, a pause in the definite present, where you could catch yourself before you dropped out of natural circulation. And then picking up speed the train set off back into the tunnel like it was heading towards the hollow darkness of the future, where things continue, without hesitation, unless you're very unlucky.

For the first time, in a carriage packed with others sharing this revelatory moment with me without even knowing it, but why would they care; or empty enough to get a seat, I was on a Tube train. There must have been this first time, a surely dramatic ceremonial moment of initiation, but what I remember more is not the train, or the line I was on, or the time I became someone who would use the Underground system, fresh blood, stepping into a hidden other world that had been moving along for decades, but a sense of not knowing what to do. The idea of this particular first time has been replaced by a generalized memory of indecision and apprehension, and unformed anticipation, about using the Tube. I didn't know where I was, which has a direct influence on your sense of who you are.

I remember once as a nineteen-year-old emerging into the fast, tireless light of what must have been Euston Underground Station, having been met off the Manchester InterCity train by a born-and-bred London friend. The Tube station was sunk under the low-slung, newly shaped and burnished main station, built with stern modernist zeal by Zurich-born architect Richard Seifert, who also designed the unloved, unmissable Centre Point skyscraper, a barely decorated vertical concrete block brutally stamped into submissive central London. Something about the discreetly glamorous setting, the severe, history-erasing glass, metal and stone of a Euston Station built where once there was hardcore but, by the early 1960s, embarrassing Victorian grandeur (boasting a famous classical arch), seemed faintly continental, although I had no way of knowing, having never been abroad.

My friend confidently escorted me down towards the ticket office, the barrier, the moving stairs, indifferent to the tangled dangling wires and scarred, low-hanging ceilings, finding the platform, on the dangerous edge of scorched metal rails slicing through a grimy soot-encrusted chasm where small animals lurk, moving as if he were completely comfortable under the city. He knew what to do and which way to go and didn't even have to look at the maps that were pasted at just the right height in just the right places along the walls, as though they were pictures of the back of his own hand, and he didn't need to keep looking at them.

The maps were covered with straight lines, made up of different very definite colours, crossing each other, knotting together, breaking apart, named and labelled as if in code, abstracting real-world London into a disciplined yet delirious pattern that seemed more cubist, or futurist, than realistically useful. You had to already be in a position of certain strength to know what this map meant, to know how it was meant to help you. If you were feeling as fragile as a newcomer, as inadequate as an outsider, the pattern of lines demanded the sort of interpreting you would surely never have the time to achieve. They represented another London altogether from the built-up place up top, one where the facts, rumours and commotion on the legendary ground above seeped below into this remote, nebulous reflection.

I couldn't understand my friend's ringing confidence. I couldn't understand how to make sense of a skeletal, collapsed version of the city that was mapped out in such cryptic form. He acted like this was the only thing he was in the mood for, and he was brilliant at it. Without even thinking, he knew the short cuts, the secret routes, the sudden, shiny tiled twists and turns, like he could see everything at a glance. I was entering pure, dashing mystery, constantly closing in around you, with the horizon never far away, one always being replaced by another. Blank faces surrounded me, offering me no clues about what they were thinking, about how many years it had been since the moment they entered this territory for the very first time.

To get to your destination, which would initially look more or less the same wherever you got off, involved negotiating a space that did not resemble any of the spaces I had got used to, growing up amidst the consolidated transport systems around Manchester, which were all above ground, give or take a few brief tunnels. In Manchester, you did not leave the streets and pavements behind, above your head, in order to get somewhere – you were always on them, or above them, on the top deck of a bus, or on a train yards-high crossing a viaduct, seeing revelations of progress, or discarded ruins, or bricked-up, boarded-over nooks and crannies, all around you. You didn't plunge down into all this rushing and pushing, this gushing of air as a train streamed in front of you on the platform, fast enough to threaten your safety, on a collision course with the next minute, before you broke back into the world above which was carrying on as though there was nothing at all underneath moving around and around A to B and back again invisibly constantly distantly rumbling.

Underground, north, south, east, west dissolved, the sky had gone, the weather had folded, day and night crossed over, and you sunk into a surreptitious time zone where the past and future took their own time and sometimes swapped roles. To this day, I see people at platform level wandering the corridors, retracing their steps, wondering which way to turn, staring, pointing, sighing at the maps, which are meant to help, tipping into panic, stymied by escalators heading the wrong way, getting in the way of those who know what they are doing, are sure of themselves, like they live down here, where the city ghosts itself, a submerged labyrinthine space broken up into ricocheting fragments, and I hear the confused ones say what I would be thinking the first few times I entered this fully functioning fantasy: how do I know where I am going, how do I get there, which way is the place I need to be? It's as though they have actually lost direction and purpose in an area where life has been reduced to nothing much other than direction and purpose.

After such an experience, your dreams become a little less safe. The lost ones find themselves abandoned in the cheerless earth, falling away from what it is to be human, and the only way out involves a form of skill and improvisation that can cope with the fact they are not in London and they are not elsewhere. They are somewhere that is as peculiar as though they were floating a few metres above packed, prodigious London, or trapped a few seconds ahead of or behind normal time, and the only solution is to get used to it. To make it seem like the most normal thing in the world, that it is not deviant to find yourself under the ground, moving about in ways that bear no relation to how you move about the city on the surface.

Quite simply, you have to know what you are doing, or leave the Underground behind, where it belongs, somewhere else. You need to quickly become a poised part of the secret organization of those that do know what they are doing; who know how to possess the land, bring imaginary skylines into being, create accurate connections out of thin air, and comfortably reach their destination where their other life can resume. You absolutely need to take the damned thing for granted.

2

Eventually, there was a Tube line I could call
my own, and learn to take for granted, simply
because of where I ended up living in London
after leaving home. There was a first time I used
the Bakerloo Line, and then there would be
hundreds of times I used it.

I knew next to nothing about how the city
so logically and illogically fitted together and
how you made your way around – above the
ground, and below. I started using the Bakerloo
during 1979 because it was the nearest line
to my first flat, in north-west London, close
to both Swiss Cottage and Finchley Road

Tube stations, right on the ragged southern edge of the NW3 district down the hill from Hampstead. It was from here that I began and ended my Tube journeys around the city, and began to work out how London was made up. The Finchley Road that streamed relentless traffic out of London towards Hendon and the M1 'gateway to the north' motorway became the centre of my London landscape, of my unfolding sense of how everything connected geographically and historically.

I began regularly travelling on the Bakerloo Line during the last few months that it actually existed as two separate lines, heading out from Baker Street Station in different directions across the unravelling, crooked northern London suburbs. One of its branches terminated at Watford after threading through Edgware Road, Maida Vale, Queen's Park, North Wembley and Harrow & Wealdstone (connecting with the mainline station opened in 1837), the other made it all the way to Stanmore via St John's Wood (for Lord's Cricket Ground),

Kilburn, Willesden Green and Wembley Park (for Wembley Stadium).

The original, more succinct and one-branch Bakerloo Line was officially opened on 10 March 1906, and named the Baker Street & Waterloo Railway. It had been built to absorb passengers and shoppers from the cluttered, congested West End of London where up on the streets there was already heavy bus traffic, the internal combustion engine beginning its intractable transformation of the twentieth century. Tunnelling three miles through the centre of London between Baker Street and Lambeth North (then called Kennington Road), actually on Westminster Bridge Road; and within months on to Elephant & Castle, taking in Oxford Circus, Piccadilly, Charing Cross and Waterloo, it passed almost directly under what would become in 1934 the BBC's permanent central offices and radio studios, Broadcasting House, and, rarely for the Underground, it ventured into south London beneath the River Thames. Workers digging the Bakerloo Thames tunnels reputedly suffered from the bends, proving the difficulties involved in penetrating south of the river.

The year that the Bakerloo began, 1906, is an arbitrary chronological zone that can help make sense of various interactions and cross-fertilizations in art and science that happened to be around at the same time, suggesting there might actually be some greater reason for all this coincidence. There was the first emergence of a working mechanical television; the first radio broadcast of audio; the invention of a vacuum tube which would lead to electronic amplification. It's when Freud's theories of the unconscious began to earn wider recognition; when composer Arnold Schoenberg, protégé of Strauss and Mahler, was almost cruelly questioning traditional tonality; the year that 27-year-old Albert Einstein was promoted to the rank of technical assistant level II at the Swiss Federal Patent office, a year after his famous 'miracle year' when he published five papers that expressed how time and space,

matter and energy, were locked together in
the most astonishing embrace; when forty-
year-old pianist, philosopher and composer
Ferruccio Busoni was writing a manifesto called
Sketch of a New Aesthetic of Music, bemoaning
the restrictions of traditional Western music,
imagining a way beyond the limitations
of notation, boldly advocating the use of
electrical sound sources; and meanwhile the
first authentic recording star, Enrico Caruso,
had finessed his singing technique in the
primitive, unamplified recording studios
of the day, uncannily and clairvoyantly
transferring something vocally intoxicating
and theatrically persuasive to early, harsh and
scratchy, quarter-inch-thick, fast-spinning
78 rpm gramophone recordings.

   An affectionate *Evening News* nickname
clipped the BS & W Railway's cumbersome
full-length name to the friendlier Baker-loo,
which quickly caught on and led to the official
hyphen-less Bakerloo and disapproval amongst
offended railway purists. (Its name was perhaps

an early newspaper-incubated ancestor of the compounding of famous supercouples' names, such as Angelina and Brad into Brangelina.)

Other lines would become known as Central, District, Circle, Northern, Metropolitan, even Piccadilly: curt, concise names that embodied a resonant administrative neutrality that could belong in a disconnected Jean-Luc Godard science-fiction film set precisely anywhere as long as it was nowhere, but even the brisk, no-nonsense Victoria Line, named after the sullen nineteenth-century 'grandmother of Europe', seemed less antiquated than the Bakerloo, with its quaint fabricated name, a word somehow shaped like a waxed ornate Edwardian moustache.

Within a year, by 1907, when the first purely synthetic plastic, Bakelite, was invented, marking the beginning of the plastics industry, and subsequent widespread plastic trivia, the Bakerloo strayed west to Marylebone and the Edgware Road. By 1913 it slipped slightly south to convoluted, besooted Paddington Station, where three years before on 20 May a dignified-looking steam train had set off for Windsor Station taking Edward VII's coffin and mourners for the Funeral Procession to St George's Chapel.

The Underground rail network in general was pushing further out of the central areas, into the mushrooming suburbs it was helping to create, hunting down potential new passengers. In 1915 the slowly lengthening Bakerloo Line abruptly turned north-west at Paddington and broke the inner-city borders, first to Queen's Park and Willesden Junction, and two years later joining up with existing overground suburban rail lines all the way to Watford, on the edge of the rest of England. It would be the system's longest line until the Piccadilly extension in 1932–3. None of these names of places changed, the routes didn't change, the journeys, destinations and connections to houses, work, shops and schools remained the same as everything else changed, stretched, accelerated, was invented, exploited and made obsolete during a cracking century that sometimes seemed on the verge of completely breaking apart, blessed, cursed and consumed by ambition, power and technology, by fear, fury and wild, temporarily satisfied desires.

In November 1939 a new tunnel was opened from Baker Street to Finchley Road, where Bakerloo trains took over a branch of the Metropolitan Line opened in 1932 through to Stanmore, creating the two Bakerloo branches. In spring of the same year, the 27-year-old Los Angeles-born arch-utopian John Cage, described by his teacher Schoenberg as 'an inventor not a composer, but an inventor of genius', performed in a Seattle radio studio *Imaginary Landscape No. 1*, one of the first compositions to include live electronics. The piece structurally blended together novel, elemental noise and familiar musical sound, creating ominous tension by combining a few piano notes, struck and stroked Chinese-cymbal rolls and crashes, tempo variations, progressively louder interior-piano-string strumming and a range of humming, wailing and weeping pitches generated by 78 rpm-frequency test recordings played on two variable-speed turntables. Cage, using this electronically balanced synthesis of music, noise and conceptual thought, was beginning to track how technology was taking over the twentieth century, producing an intensifying combination of anxiety and euphoria.

My most regular journey on the soon-to-be-extinct Stanmore branch of the Bakerloo was fairly brief. I would join it, sometimes at open-air Finchley Road yards before it entered the raw, gaping tunnel going south after an outdoor overground journey from Stanmore, or at the next station, Swiss Cottage, where it was now fully embedded into the subterranean Tube system. This essentially is where the Tube becomes the Tube, even though most of the networks tracks are not underground. The Tube is the Tube in another place deeply distant from the everyday sky-high sun, clouds, moon and stars, where you think about things differently, where you can be in different places

that all look the same, surrounded by others,
who've also become something else – so they
are strangers anyway, and then even stranger,
because they are temporarily concealed, passive,
face to face, back to back, people in, people out,
crushed together, touching, pulling away, lost for
words, between the lines, not quite themselves,
not quite anchored, temporarily fixed in this
volatile, secluded zone, fellow nomads, people
in, people out, at the mercy of invisible forces,
keeping their minds well away from the dense,
braced and soaking, rat-packed worm-jammed
void that encircles them.

3

The Bakerloo Line does not have the sexiest
of reputations, and a large amount of this is
down to the colour it ended up being on the
brilliant, lit-up Tube map. The colour that
formally represents the Bakerloo line on the
London Underground system is basic brown.
It could be described not unfairly as quite a dull
brown. It's not a brown exotically radiating out
of orange, it's not an alluring reddish brown, or
a tantalizing yellowish brown, edging towards
gold; it's not the umber seventeenth- and
eighteenth-century artists might have used to
realistically portray warm, ethereal atmosphere,

or as part of their scrupulous palette to capture elusive flesh tones; it's not the dour, provisional brown of the early cubists, but something very safely, dependably brown.

It's barely changed since the faceless colour committee originally selected it in 1908 when the first map of the Underground was designed and the Bakerloo conclusively became brown, a very early twentieth-century brown, which brings something of the nineteenth century with it – the colour of Sherlock Holmes's pipe, a Gladstone bag, a grandfather clock. An unexciting, stout brown built to do a tough job on behalf of an organization, a department; to methodically absorb smoke, nicotine, fog, stains and open fires. In India, brown is the colour of mourning, because it is the colour of dying leaves. The Japanese tend not to use an abstract word to represent colour but descriptive compound words that capture particular shades: tea colour (*chai-ro*), fox colour, fallen leaf. Bakerloo brown is carpet colour, corduroy colour, cow colour, fake tan. It's not chocolate square – there's something flavourless about it. Actually, it's earth colour. It's a colour that comes out of the earth, from soil, dirt, mud, peat: it is, really, the earth that's all around the tunnel as it burrows under the centre of London, boring its way through the muck and mire like a mole out of hell.

In the first decades of the twentieth century, you can imagine it being a relatively fashionable colour, but by the late 1970s, when I started regularly using the Bakerloo Line, it was considered old-fashioned, even kitsch, the result of various damaging associations that had accumulated through the century. It had become a colour that no one would particularly choose; one they end up with, when all other options had been exhausted.

Perhaps it was first caught out, somehow overruled, by the artistic and spiritual eruption of colour that peaked in 1910. This was when art critic and artist Roger Fry organized an exhibition at London's Grafton Galleries of eclectic, visionary, then largely unknown French painters from the previous three decades who were each exploring ways to go around and beyond increasingly conservative, mid-nineteenth-century Impressionism. Some of them had been known as Impressionists themselves (including Cezanne and Pissarro), but by the 1880s started to feel that the term itself, which most of the artists loathed, and the painting style that supposedly connected a visceral, interpretative way of using paint was limiting their artistic progress. Once the idea of Impressionism hinted at greater freedoms, it was hard to stop there, and what once seemed fantastically new quickly seemed a dead end.

The compositional innovations, enriched colour and subject matter of the Impressionists pointed towards what was about to come, a further breaking up and breaking down of tradition, an extreme dismantling of representation and form, something that couldn't really be labelled, and therefore controlled and tamed, but which needed some form of naming, so that it could become the

24

kind of observed, recorded movement that reportage and history can deal with.

Under pressure from a journalist demanding convenient collective identification for his exhibition, Fry spontaneously labelled the obliquely connected art obsessively anticipating abstraction 'post-Impressionism'. The mainstream audience and much of the art establishment were still troubled by the way the Impressionists had apparently jettisoned traditional painting methods; they were avant-garde enough. Post-Impressionism in transcendental pursuit of a modern art for modern times stretched convention to breaking point, took too many liberties with perspective and subject matter, and was fearfully labelled 'anarchic and degenerate'.

Fry's biographer and stark modernist Virginia Woolf, not usually a fan of arbitrary judgements, responded to the exhibition in 1924 with uncharacteristic non-reticent hyperbole by announcing that this was the moment when 'human character changed'.

It was the extreme colour of late-nineteenth-century Impressionism taken even further by early-twentieth-century post-Impressionism that broke through the general resistance. The radiant, exultant colours of Cezanne, Gauguin, Van Gogh and Kandinsky, representing a conceptual shift in how art could define reality and spirit, spread through fashion and commercial art into a wider culture and made brown seem glum or plain old hat. Those flaring, broken-up post-Impressionist colours and the associated fracturing and reshaping of reality blazed through the twentieth century, into cinema, television, advertising, art, design and pop culture, pushing mere modest brown down into the ground.

At the worst extreme, there is the memory of the Nazi brown shirts – actually khaki, originally intended for German soldiers in Africa and cheaply bought in bulk by the Nazi Party – the Brown Revolution in 1933 when the Nazis seized power, and their Brown House national headquarters in Munich, which lends the word a particularly shabby if not extremely shitty dimension. This is without mentioning the surname of Adolf Hitler's mistress, Eva.

Less toxically, but not adding to any potential glamour, brown was typically the colour of healthy, wholesome, ultimately bland food, a bit hippy, a bit worthy. Less healthily, the gluey instant gravy containing fly-sized powder lumps dunked on to wretched school dinners of sweaty, bloated, pock-marked sausages did not help the idea of brown. What great football team wore brown? Taste-changing, agenda-setting punks did not wear brown: it was the colour of a prog-rock guitarist's flared loon pants, his shapeless Afghan coat, his baggy tie-dyed granny vest, the apocryphal colour of the acid at the Woodstock Festival in 1969 that the MC and Grateful Dead's house clown Wavy Gravy warned from the stage caused the bad trips, even if it was the warning itself that freaked people out.

If it wasn't the colour of their uniform, those who wore brown clothing in daily life seemed to lack distinct purpose, or be slyly wearing a non-aligned disguise to cover up their true, unruly passions. Because it was so down to earth, no-nonsense corporations would use it to brand their companies as sensible and reliable. You could have electric blue, but never electric brown. 'Brown is a colour that no one likes,' mused exacting Italian fashion designer Miuccia Prada, 'so of course I like it, because it is difficult.'

Dingy, non-impudent Bakerloo brown seemed an old, traditional colour. It was a self-effacing, even camouflaged reminder that the Underground system, in many ways as flash, as fresh, as the future; transport that could actually transport the mind; a place where everything is always beginning, was a classic, heroic late-nineteenth-century enterprise, initially sniffily dismissed by *Punch* magazine as 'the sewer railway', made out of ancient wood and primitive materials as much as modern metal and clean lines; once, amazingly, powered by steam.

4

I'd come down to London at the end of 1978,
and rented a room with my girlfriend, Karen, in
a basic two-bedroom first-floor flat planted in the
amorphous, routinely residential area of north-
west London down the hill from the Finchley
Road that could, depending on which way
you approached it, be called West Hampstead,
Kilburn or Swiss Cottage. I had been in London
on my own a few times a year or two before
I moved, and used the Tube to get around, but I
can't remember which lines I went on, except
that the first one I used was definitely not the
Bakerloo. I attended a one-day music festival

at Hyde Park featuring a bill topped by the temporary ACNE collective containing Kevin Ayers, John Cale, Nico and Brian Eno; I went to see Patti Smith play her first British shows, two nights at the London Roundhouse, sleeping cold and rough overnight in a park in Hendon; saw Manchester group Buzzcocks play their first gig in central London; and went for an interview with the editor of the *New Musical Express*, Nick Logan, high up in the squarely practical Richard Seifert-designed King's Reach Tower, concretely lodged on the banks of the Thames opposite St Paul's Cathedral, which led to me writing for the paper a few months before my twentieth birthday.

For about eighteen months I wrote for them from Manchester, before achieving what had been my dream job since the age of fourteen: writing full-time in London for the *NME*, which I loved because it made such stunning sense as an inspiring, path-finding guide to music, and also as a beacon, a manual containing all kinds of vital information about what to do with yourself in a world that seemed

out of reach. At the time, to music fans born say
at the end of the 1950s and in the early 1960s,
a telephone in your house was relatively new,
and there was only one model to choose from;
and television was three-channelled, barely
in colour, hardly broadcasting during the day,
never overnight. The video recorder was years
away, and you watched what was on at whatever
time it was on, with absolutely no chance of
seeing programmes or films on tv whenever you
wanted.

There were no celebrity-gossip magazines,
give or take the quaint *Carry On* crudity of
Titbits, and there were the early stirrings
of a dominant tabloid mentality but nothing
that you thought would necessarily take
over and operate as an aggressive kind of
cultural dictatorship. The relentlessly cheerful,
suspiciously over-friendly Radio 1 was still
only a few years old, a carefully calculated
late-1960s BBC reaction to the needs of a new
generation desperate to escape the atmosphere
of restriction and decay that still infected the

country after the catastrophic fallout of the Second World War.

In the mid-1970s we were much closer to the end of the Second World War than those of us in our teens at the time ever really appreciated. Everything seemed as modern as the world should be, because it was as up to date as anything had ever been. We were already a primitive model of the global village; the Beatles had been and gone, having considerably adjusted various cultural and commercial parameters; we had electricity and comedy heroes; and there were pop stars and rock stars and film greats and television wonders. There was plenty of stuff going on to ensure that thirty, forty or years later there would be much nostalgic swooning at how simple and wonderful things used to be, when the young were beginning to make their voices heard and their feelings permanently felt. But we were in a kind of shock, because of what had been happening during the twentieth century: the wars, the revolutions, the assassinations, the serial killers, the inventions, the political shenanigans and battles, the recessions, the fragmentation and disorder, the stale culture, the urgent, disorientating post-war reconstruction and an impulsive obsession with uninviting modernization, the Berlin Wall and the red book of Mao, the facile shine of the American dream and the demonized remoteness of the Soviet Union. It wasn't a time to look back, nostalgia wasn't a major motivational force, because to look back meant the war, and the war before that, and the future seemed more of a place where you might find safety, rather than the apparently ruined past. In the middle of all this disturbance and realignment, the weekly *New Musical Express* was like an encyclopaedic combination of *Monty Python*, MTV, Google, Spotify and Amazon shaken up with a little HBO and Twitter, when all those things seemed to be smashing frontiers and opening up new freedoms.

Irreverent, playful, ideological, smart, provocative and experimental music papers

were then – along with vigilant, loner disc jockeys
such as John Peel – where, if you were anything
like me, you found and made up personal, fluid
maps of fast-moving, fast-changing rock music
that enabled you to discover ideas and sounds
that fitted into and symbolized your life and
mind – the life of your mind. Rock writers,
with a semi-crazed, self-regulated sense of
responsibility, found a new role in sorting through
this rapid, regenerating progress, explaining and
exploring it as if the music was a way not only
of replacing history, which had been in trouble
since the war, but of generating the future itself.
Everything was taken very seriously, with a kick
of the combatively ideological, the seductively
facetious. Your favourite musicians and pop stars –
Bowie, Bolan, Jagger, Iggy, Ferry – spoke through
them, through the charged, hypersensitive, quasi-
literary writing of rock journalists influenced
by Norman Mailer, Tom Wolfe, Nick Tosches,
Thomas Pynchon, Jack Kerouac, Susan Sontag,
William Burroughs and J. G. Ballard, because
there was nowhere else for them to speak.

The *New Musical Express* was delivered into rusty grey, quite out-of-the-way and out-of-work Stockport and into my impatient, needy hands every Thursday during the early- to mid-1970s – coming out of the tunnel of last week, heading towards the tunnel of next week, releasing light, difference and meaning into the static, lustreless present – and very quickly the thought of writing for it became for me the thing that mattered most. I didn't want to be a pop star, I wanted to write about pop stars, but it seemed highly unlikely that a lost, naive, traditionally provincial teenage boy with little going for him but wild enthusiasm, an appetite for uncommon sensation and a secretly nurtured fascination with the outlandishly obscure would actually end up in what was for all its elastic wit and intoxicating inside knowledge a professional organization established in London. It acted like it was a subversive continuation of the underground magazines of the late 1960s such as *International Times* and *Oz*, but it was actually owned by IPC – International Publishing

Company – which also published *Horse and Hound*, *Country Life* and *Woman's Own*.

Timing played a part in opening the doors of the *NME* – real journalism, in the real world – to people like me, loosely connected to the world only through pop music, television and books. Untrained as a journalist, leaving school at sixteen, teaching myself to write based on the things I read – which included cocky, self-invented rock writers, especially American ones often acting like they were as much Warhol, Billy the Kid, Rimbaud, Ginsberg and Dylan as they were Hemingway, Mailer, Wolfe and Hunter S. Thompson – there was really only one place I could end up as any kind of journalist.

Punk rock erupted, a jagged, domestic intensification of a variety of agitating post-war revolutionary ideas, manifesting itself as a dramatic call to action during a time of intense uncertainty, but also as tremendously deviant show business. British rock music had up to that point, with the influence of newfangled post-war

American music, been a ravishing, freedom-
seeking replenishment of eccentric, energizing
music-hall spirit. Punk added to this flamboyant
hybrid of entertainment and purpose a charged
ideological edge. It was still full of show, of
glamorous, sometimes humorous, appeal, but
it also had an accusatory effervescence, even a
revolutionary fervour.

I was the right age in the right north-west
city staggering under its own history – about to
break free, retaining its own accent – with the
right aggregate of eccentric qualifications to
find a way into the paper; a self-built knowledge
of the history and importance of rock music
and an uncompromising belief that punk rock
as an attitude really mattered. To outsiders,
sceptics and outright cynics, punk seemed a
noisy, snotty-nosed mess of spite and spitting;
for those on the inside of an outsider scene
changing shape by the day, it was something
liberating, even noble, an art movement with
a disruptive, psyched-up soundtrack. Amidst
a tense, nervous world, a battered, fading

landscape, filled with shabby, unsightly town centres and morose, changeless suburbs, and a general sense of spiritual failure, it suddenly seemed you could make up the future using new sounds, new energy and your imagination. Punk, the way it recommended an experimental mentality, helped me to become a writer, if only because I could demonstrate self-invented expertise in this distinctive new hybrid of music, fashion and social planning.

After moving to north London – north, I always said, in case I needed to make a quick getaway back up to Manchester – the Bakerloo became the line on which most Mondays in 1979 I would take my typewritten pages to where the *NME* offices had moved from the sterile, demoralizing and corporate-seeming King's Reach Tower. They were now along Carnaby Street, drifting a little after a hyped-up 60s fashion high, near Oxford Circus Tube, past remnants of London history represented by the grand Palladium Theatre and proud, half-timbered Liberty store, which helped invent the theatrical idea of modern commerce. (When I was living in Stockport, I would post my articles, sticking a picture of the Queen on to envelopes containing passionate, highly topical reviews of the Sex Pistols, Throbbing Gristle and Stiff Little Fingers. Once or twice a piece would get lost. I didn't keep a copy and my diligently prepared words about Richard Hell, the Normal or the Adverts, painstakingly punched out on a cheap manual typewriter with no delete, spell check or cut and paste and a worn ribbon mostly drained of ink, would be abandoned for ever.)

I'd read on the Tube the features and reviews that I'd written often through Sunday night, with no sleep, to check them, and even revel in them; the idea I was meeting Blondie, Clash, Siouxsie Sioux, the Stranglers, even – Jesus Christ – Patti Smith, and could legitimately call myself a writer. Then I would hand them in, to those quiet, driven heroes who turned these sheets of paper into *NME* articles. Two days later I would return on the Bakerloo, and see the piece printed in the paper, with my byline, which never ceased to astonish me, taking it back on the Tube to read what was now published, where sometimes it was the cover story, and inside took up four or five pages of the music paper I still loved.

My only criterion then about the length of my features and interviews when there was no real editorial directive – the paper daringly chasing the sort of energy that word limits would hinder – was that I liked to hand in about twelve or thirteen A4 pages of closely spaced text, which for some self-deluding reason I had decided was about 3,000 words. It was only years later I realized those pieces were at their very least 5,000 words, letters tapped one by one on to the page with little chance of altering their pattern. A few would go on even longer, even the ones about the obscure, enthralling Vic Godard, Peter Hammill, Howard Devoto or Kevin Coyne, where my enthusiasm took me past the point of no return. They still, for better or worse, made it into print more or less intact.

Some of these articles, which flirted with being essays striving to detect hidden cultural patterns, or were exuberant diary entries, or worked-up blasts of confession and excitement, would seem to be about one thing, and then, half way through, start to be about something else altogether. There would be complaints – one lengthy feature I wrote after travelling to Los Angeles on a first visit to America to write about costumed pop surrealists Devo caused some to ask, why are you writing a piece about Los Angeles that seems to actually be about Devo, and others to ask, on the other hand, about the same piece, why are you writing a piece about Devo that seems to actually be about Los Angeles? By the end of such pieces, though, I liked to think, it all made sense – maybe that piece wasn't about either Los Angeles or Devo but something else altogether, that came from adding together Los Angeles, Devo and me on a first visit to America – and the journey might not have got there in a direct way, but the route it took was a little more scenic, a little more

41

revealing than it might have been had it taken a more direct, or predictable, route.

Sometimes on a journey, it's good to suddenly change your mind about where you are going, and how you are getting there. Even if you do follow an established route, and go straight to where you are heading, the best journey is all about changing your mind, which helps you find out where and who you actually are, which may then help others on their own journeys, looking for their own direction, their own destination.

5

On 30 April 1979, the Bakerloo services from
Baker Street to Stanmore were withdrawn, and
the very next day transferred to the new Jubilee
Line, connecting with additional tunnelling
south of Baker Street that terminated at
Charing Cross. North of Baker Street, the
new Jubilee Line still used the stiff, ornamental,
brown-and-cream tiled-and-wooden 1939
Bakerloo stations at Swiss Cottage and St John's
Wood, and the only new platforms built for
the glossy new line were at Bond Street, Green
Park and Charing Cross – which closed as a
Jubilee stop twenty years later when the line

was expensively extended, in a much more prestigiously spacious, glisteningly glass-and-steel, family-friendly-futurist manner, to Stratford in east London in time for the end-of-Millennium celebrations.

The Jubilee inherited the timeworn pre-war northern Bakerloo stations, but took from the Bakerloo their relatively sleek and metallic 1972 stock trains, which even though they were based on a 1967 design looked as though they belonged in a world where there had actually been a moon landing, nuclear tests, platform shoes, decimalization and a film called *2001: A Space Odyssey*. The Bakerloo was compelled to use only its remaining ageing, shabby 1938 stock, which looked like they had begun life in a black-and-white Hitchcock murder mystery when ten Woodbine cigarettes cost 5*d*. butlers still served masters and 'A Nightingale Sang in Berkeley Square' was written. At first, on the recently unwrapped Jubilee, everything seemed more or less as it was, as the Bakerloo once had those newer trains. The platform was the same, the rail lines the same, the miles of interconnected tunnels could never be anything else, now a permanent physical part of the body of London whatever surgery, violence or embellishment was performed on the city's simmering widescreen surface.

Before the launch of the Jubilee, I'd travel four or five stops south on the Bakerloo – now a Tube regular, closing in on taking it for granted, understanding how it worked, what frame of mind you needed to be in once you were on the Tube, a combination of deeply focused and slightly adrift, where you could let your mind wander. I'd get off at Oxford Circus, materializing back outside, a few yards higher, a certain amount freer – or less free? – on the mostly known streets of London, a much more cogent if chaotic physical embodiment of communal history, of law, order, economy, conformity, where your thoughts connected for a moment or two with what you thought down there, if you hadn't completely left those thoughts behind, and then slowly dissolved into something else altogether as you reverted to your other self, the earthbound you. You begin to make sense or no sense at all of those desires that leaked into your being when you were in that other part of the city, the one that is under the ground.

Selfishly speaking, once the Jubilee replaced the Stanmore branch of the Bakerloo, the main, irritating practical difference was that my journey from north-west London to Oxford Circus was now in two parts. The new line forced me to change my accustomed route, which involved a change; change always leads to more change. I would take the Jubilee from Finchley Road or Swiss Cottage with what could sometimes seem suspiciously like an eternity of bumpy travel after St John's Wood, as if we had perhaps taken a jolting detour into an unmarked tunnel heading back in time, tasked with solving some deep-set mystery, and then finally present and near correct I would need to remember to get off at Baker Street. I would cross the platform a few yards to the conveniently placed Bakerloo Line, which had become the one spindly branch dropping down from Watford Junction. (By 1982, Bakerloo trains to Watford had been reduced to four peak-time trains, and then they were stopped altogether, leaving Queen's Park as the primary northern terminus with some trips to Stonebridge Park, along the North Circular Road, before services five stations north to Harrow & Wealdstone were reinstated in 1984, completing the standard one-branch Bakerloo route.)

My Bakerloo trip, where I'd carry my words about music and me and various mental maps of possible adventures, had been trimmed to two stops. First, the short one to the barely there, barely used Regent's Park – which is definitely not there above ground, being one of the few Tube stations with no surface buildings. You enter using inconspicuous stairways courteously descending under the Euston Road pavement alongside Regent's Park into what the hell lies within – with its deserted, melancholy platforms encased in oleaginous Edwardian tiling misting up with the ghostly tears of stranded tourists and its name mournfully picked out in brown rectangles. From there, heading south, jerkily swooping into tangled Oxford Circus, skirting the plumbed foundations of the BBC, where offbeat Pied Piper John Peel lurked, the blood and flesh of civilization seemed to rush back into the proceedings – represented by the incongruous, lustrous ox-blood tiles encasing one corner of the otherwise blandly robust Oxford Circus Station.

Psychologically, there was a difference between the lines, even if solely because of their assigned colour. The Jubilee was during its development set to be called the Fleet Line – nicely neutral and faintly futuristic, in fact named after the lost, shrunken subterranean River Fleet, reduced by the seventeenth century from Roman-era surface dash to grungy sewer duties, by the twentieth century to a buried ooze, rising at Hampstead Heath, dropping down via Camden and King's Cross, joining the Thames in a discreet spurt of relief at Blackfriars Bridge opposite King's Reach Tower. The Underground colour of the Fleet Line was destined to be grey, based on the naval meaning of the word 'fleet'. After years of planning, its name was changed to Jubilee (still approximately clinical and civic enough to satisfy Godard's filmic urges) to honour the 1977 Queen's Silver Jubilee anniversary as part of a whimsical but apparently attractive Conservative promise during that year's Greater London Council elections. The battleship grey therefore shifted to spaceship silver – the colour of speed, the greatest invention of the entire twentieth century, which kept doggedly accelerating until one century slammed into the next, creating significant historical concussion – and this was calculated to make the sailing-ship Bakerloo brown seem even more dated and forlorn.

The Bakerloo, though, retained a form of ragged, plucky majesty in the face of this glittery silver upstart. It was not completely exiled into the dust-coated moth-eaten margins by this slick new line glibly appropriating dubious Royal glory and immense investment, stealing the brown line's smarter, cleaner trains and consigning it to an eternal, loopy run via scruffy, preoccupied Paddington to the increasingly charmless and run-down north-western outskirts of London. Here, wounded district succeeded wounded district as if simply to demonstrate slovenly, perhaps aggressively absent, civic planning. The Bakerloo even darted south of the river, but not very far considering all that effort getting under the mighty Thames, perversely pulling up short a mile or so later at Elephant & Castle before it could get stuck into the endless, uncharted mostly no-Tube land beyond, and whatever sticky range of zonal black holes, but this was enough to add frayed marks of scruffiness to its reputation. (Plans to extend the southern end of the Bakerloo to poorly served profoundly south Camberwell were suspended during the Second

World War, temporarily revived, and then reduced to an occasional often politically driven rumour, a mere pipe dream. Some favoured an equally fanciful extension via Peckham to Lewisham, even beyond via Streatham to Croydon, where south London finally petered out, almost becoming another hectic, neo-futuristic city, stunted but purposefully studded with high-rise office blocks, ring roads, car parks, shopping centres and flyovers. These hypothetical southern extensions of the Bakerloo contain routes and journeys that will never happen in a lost London existing outside the phantom space of the existing Tube structure.)

In between the battered, dispossessed northern suburbs slipping between the cracks and the mostly marooned, possibly infernal south of the river; away from the mainline stations of Paddington, Marylebone and Waterloo, relentlessly loading the line with those on a mission and those not that sure, the Bakerloo's central-London relationship with royal

Regent's Park, shop-stunned Oxford Circus, stately, sweeping Regent Street and illuminated, Eros-topped Piccadilly; its passing affair with airier, affluent Maida Vale, made it seem like it was awkwardly straining to live above its station. But through it all the humiliated, scorned Bakerloo carried on, chin up, roughly charming, secure about its position in the greater scheme of things, which contained a certain sacred significance, however bad things looked on the streets, across torn strips of wasteland, around blighted estates, gaunt urban parks, still cemeteries with life on hold, row upon row of densely packed, identical humble housing, mass-produced office buildings, staunch corner pubs, cadaverous warehouses, unearthly rail depots built on the sites of former power stations; miles apart from London's major monuments, its secret centres of power and devious images of authority.

I really missed the Bakerloo now it wasn't my local line. The Bakerloo had an atmosphere all of its own, perhaps rooted in an affinity for the marginalized picked up around the Harlesden section of its roaming, in its undeniable experience; and I wasn't completely taken in by the flighty, suddenly available, wet-behind-the-ears Jubilee, which promised the future, but didn't yet deliver. I'd developed some sort of quiet love for the Bakerloo, perhaps precisely because it was as soft, cosy and familiar in its threadbare way as a floppy brown slipper, and there was something impressive about the way it was so firmly connected with the origins of the Underground system, with the very first audacious murmurings that such a ridiculous excavating enterprise demanding spectacular feats of earth moving, space generating and structural engineering was truly possible.

The Bakerloo carried with it not only broken-hearted memories of two world wars, and the dubious, even vicious peace that followed; the crushed hopes and dreams of all those that had used the line for seven decades; and the sour scents and other lingering traces of the toxic, intangible smoke that was always taking shape and fading away into itself inside the carriages and on the platforms in the days when smoking was a natural, relaxing, even sensuous part of travelling. There was more to the Bakerloo than the sense of life and time taking its toll and leaving its mark that it took with it from all those journeys up and down through the neglected, flagging, interlaced north-west regions and the terminal, mangled Elephant & Castle, surely a hideout for mutants, tramps and outcasts, which seemed closer to concrete-cast, almost apocalyptic Soviet Bloc desolation than any familiar red bus, Tower Bridge postcard image of London. South of the river had largely been left off the map, dumped down there, like waste; an afterthought, drifting outside the standard identity of the city.

The Bakerloo after all was a sturdy, surviving monument to the frontier mentality of those who first proposed a London Underground system that would ingeniously exploit capital, technology and technical reason in order to keep people moving from task to task, from place to place, from time to time as if their very netherworld movement was the motor driving surface London. It had once been utterly modern, the very latest development in the schemes and dreams of those showmen, workers and wheeler-dealer entrepreneurs making up the contours, mood and motion of a great city, fashioning unbroken and unbreakable interior connections between the past and the present. The Bakerloo was a magnificent part of the machinery of the city, an early demonstration of how visiting a city, getting round a city, moving up and down inside it, depended on machinery; how a city was made by its machinery.

Now that it was so closely connected to the youngest line, the current latest development in a fixed, adaptive system that symbolized as much as anything the unyielding complexity and alchemy of London, the Bakerloo continued to play a part in all the haphazard forward momentum and endless maintenance of spirit, exchange and purpose. The common brown Bakerloo from the olden days was in operational and existential harmony with the silver Jubilee of tomorrow: a scant few steps separated them at Baker Street, and the silver would not have existed without the brown. The meat-and-potatoes brown helped generate the circumstances and opportunities that eventually led to the supersonic silver. The Bakerloo of flaky peeling paint and deteriorating intensity was intimately connected with the newest addition to the system.

The fact that both could exist – one having shed its skin, lost a limb, to enable the other – was part of the prismatic glory of the overall network, representing an essential part of the shifting patterns of history where the past constantly coincided with the present; where both could happen at the same time; and where the survival and modification of parts of the distant past were an essential if more fragile element in the formation of the future. The Bakerloo bringing with it the ebbing, perishable

sound and vision of the early part of the
twentieth century, haunted by the century itself,
all of the triumphs, ruins, inventions, chaos,
transformation, traumas and destruction – and
much that was tedious and nothing much in
particular – carved out the future as much
as any of the more obviously fashionable,
contemporary arrivals, mechanisms, campaigns,
projects and attitudes.

6

A few months after my regular journey from
Swiss Cottage to Oxford Circus and back
again required a change halfway, my girlfriend,
Karen, brought me a present from Japan,
where she had been working. She bought me
a brand-new piece of machinery made by
Sony, which at the time seemed unimaginably
of the future – perhaps as much as the Tube
system did when it first opened. In the mid-1970s,
Sony were mostly known for selling what
seemed the most desirable television sets,
especially their sleek Trinitron, which was
a considerable advance from the chunky

wood-grain brown-box TV sets rented from the local Granada shop, then as much a fixture on the high street as Poundland, William Hill and Starbucks would be forty years later.

Colour television had started transmission on BBC 2 in 1967, and on ITV and BBC 1 two years later, but didn't become common in British homes until the early 1970s. Those who had a white Trinitron in their homes were on the frictionless monorail to the future of the world. Aesthetically, the Trinitron was light years ahead of anything else, certainly on the swish, minimal outside: like the bewitching range of Apple iDevices would be decades later. There was a confident nakedness about its design, an elimination of unnecessary features compared to previous products that fussily boasted on the outside about their technology, and it anticipated in its unadorned simplicity the computer monitors that were about to invade planet Earth.

The new, more portable, 'made in Japan' Sony gadget brought back for me had not yet officially reached Britain, or even America, and so possibly I had one of the first if not the very first example in London of what had been made available in Japan on 1 July 1979 – selling only 3,000 in the first month, as though people didn't initially know what to make of it – two months after the opening of the Jubilee Line, when the idea of Japanese hi-tech miniaturization had yet to achieve global impact.

Karen bought me a Sony Walkman, with the model number TPS-L2, able to play, but not record on, cassettes, in stereo, with relatively decent sound quality. The Walkman featured the Sony logo as seen on the Trinitron, lettering designed in 1955, the year it was registered as a trademark (months before the first Sony-labelled product, a pocket-sized radio), perfected by 1973, and still in use today. 'Sony' had no particular meaning in Japanese, building on an idea of something exotically local to a Japan that did not actually exist, a fantasy Japan intended to replace the fallen image of Japan distressing the popular imagination for one reason or another after the Second World War.

'Sony' was an imaginary word chosen with self-fulfilling perception to sound like something that in the future would belong on the world's billboards with Coca-Cola, Kodak, IBM, and Mercedes; and that's what it became with the help of the Walkman. Once the Walkman, as a great performance, a piece of entertainment in its own right, gave Sony a greater aura, occupying a larger amount of the consumer's mind, beyond purely being the remote, indistinct provider of electronic devices, it exploited its increasingly intimate technological grip to diversify beyond electronics and become an entertainment empire.

Neat and tidy, if hissy and fragile, cassettes possessed a plastic dinkiness that verged on the toylike, but there was also something mysteriously sophisticated and definitely capable about them. They were then in the process of seeing off bloated, colourless eight-track cartridges as a format for pre-recorded music, having become the main commercial support for the vinyl album. Cassettes themselves were a relatively young format; introduced in 1963 by the Dutch electronics company Philips, mainly for dictating machines, pre-recorded album cassettes were introduced commercially in Europe at the end of 1965. This was forty years after the introduction of electrical recording, and the transferring of sound-wave patterns into electricity, the very beginnings of unlimited amplification – previously, there had been no method of turning a small sound into a bigger one for the purpose of recording it.

Eight tracks, originally conceived as futuristic-seeming music capsules for use on private Learjets, unravelled into extinction, heading towards a comical legacy by the early 1980s. The cassette nimbly carried on, the main other format next to the compact disc that supplanted the vinyl record by the late 1980s. At the time the Walkman was manufactured, there was no sign that the cassette would last as a major, mainstream part of pop culture for only a few more years. There seemed no way that one day they would appear as retro quaint as the thick, brittle 78 rpm disc, mourned by certain obsessive audio fetishists, in a world where people pulled, grazed and flicked their music out of an illusory cloud and slipped it into invisible compartments linked in commercially administered space: cassettes were versatile, attractive, quite stylish alternatives to vinyl, with an ineffable sound quality as likely to encourage romantic affection, and seemed as likely to be outmoded as electricity itself. The cassette, the word itself suggesting something enticingly compressed and novel, seemed to be part of a glistening future that would never fade away.

By 1989, the cassette was at the peak of its success, not least because cheap, handy, blank cassettes were the perfect way of compiling, home taping and sharing with others your own selection of music – exactly the appeal of the cassette that would become a problem by the mid-1990s when record companies became particularly paranoid about easily copied, pirated music, especially in those countries where they were not established. In the late 1980s a self-labelled collection of cassettes containing fussed-over compilations of your favourite music was closer than your album collection to the eventual idea of a vast library of songs on your iPod.

The Walkman, released into a less complicated, less pernicious entertainment landscape, would become known as the world's first low-cost portable music device. Its branding alone was novel – it had a name, it wasn't only a tape player or recorder, or a radio, it was a Walkman, with a metallic hint of the robotic, which suggested it was more than what it seemed, with its own separate, sophisticated identity, which you could absorb into your own, to enhance and modify it. There was form, and function, and convenience, which were not intrinsically ground-breaking outside the size and lightness, but there was this greater, seductive dimension of significance and personality, and of it becoming an integral part of your own personal world, and how you expressed yourself.

It was a little smaller than a paperback book, so therefore not much bigger than a cassette, which seemed some sort of miracle – that the workings required to power the machine and produce the sound could be incorporated into such a compact casing. Perhaps the most significant thing, along with the revolutionary removal of an internal loudspeaker, was the 50 gram, or 1.7 ounce, weight of the headphones, which were in scale with the player itself, replacing the usual eight-times-as-heavy, bulbous, ear-covering headphones. You could now take music with you wherever you went, and somehow, at the time, even though there were machines that could have done this job, and there had been tiny transistor radios for years, this seemed incredibly exciting. Not least because you couldn't take a radio on the Tube, if you wanted to, because there would be no signal.

The Walkman also enabled you to choose

the music you wanted to hear – part of the overall freedom of movement that it introduced which mechanized and symbolized other forms of industrialized emotional and physical freedoms that had changed what it meant to be young. This machine represented how you could be in control of your own destiny and the personal details of that destiny in ways that would have been unimaginable a hundred years, even twenty years, before. It was a classic example of how pieces of technological product became the catalysts of significant social change, encouraging uses not predicted by the companies that developed and mass-produced them.

The Walkman was a conceptual product that helped you conceptualize your own life, something that helped take you on a voyage somewhere new, into a constantly unfolding landscape of the future. Nothing would come close to replacing it for two decades, when Apple, with methodical, colonizing purpose superbly disguised as progressive, reforming flair, embedded the iPod and MP3 player into a whole elaborate system of music, self-image and pleasure that it could actually control, organize and edit from within to the point of manipulating reality and identity.

The Walkman was the very first hint of a world to come, in the then moderately distant and relatively opaque twenty-first century, where what you played your music on would become central to the experience, to the extent that the product – upgraded latest model rapidly replacing upgraded latest model – would become as famous and fashionable, if not more so, as your favourite pop stars and musicians. People started to collect experiences rather than things, and used technology to generate and record these experiences. The machine itself, as much as what was on it, was how you presented your hip, knowing credentials to the world. The machine itself was what soothed cultural anxieties, refreshed your identity, and actually articulated how you resisted the conformity of imposed lifestyles and mass-culture tastes – even

as you were obediently reacting to a carefully
targeted and marketed trend that purported
to be helping you break free of commercial
pressure. The Walkman, then, on and around
autumn 1979, on the Bakerloo Line deep
beneath Broadcasting House, home of the
BBC, where John Peel with lazy, picky genius
presented his rambling, furtively didactic late-
night radio show, set off a chain of commands
that changed human behaviour.

Not only did I consider myself the first person
to own the fabulously cool new Walkman player,
and to show it off to astounded friends and
colleagues, who could delicately hold the future
in their hands as though it might shatter at any
moment, but I also imagined that I was the first
person to sit on the Tube listening to music of
my own choosing through wonderfully light
and transportable stereo headphones. At least,
I make the claim to be the first person to listen
to music on the Tube through headphones on
a Sony Walkman, detached from reality even
within the detachment from reality of being on

the Tube: the very first instance of what thirty
years later would be completely unsurprising
and normal. In 1979, this way of being wired
for, or to, sound, was science fiction. You could
speculate but it seemed Star Trek far-fetched
that one day you could use devices like this
made by companies like Sony as phones you
could slip into your pocket and use on the move
around the city, making calls, sending messages,
grading product, playing electronic games – on
your own and with others – checking facts on
some epic encyclopaedic guidebook, watching
television, even contributing to unfolding
worldwide debates and dwelling on details at
motionless speed as if you were a central part
of the latest event – Brainees they might be
called, Smarties, or Phoneys.

I was in the future as far as it had got on
the Bakerloo Line in 1979 as I pulled out of
Baker Street, on my way to the *NME* offices,
taking this small minimally decorated silver-
and-blue metal box with its orange button,
two headphone jacks, and soon-to-be-obsolete

'hotline button' for cutting out the music
and talking with the presumed other listener,
into the brown Bakerloo province. (Sony was
anxious that making the Walkman exclusively
for one would seem to encourage unwelcome
isolation, and included the second headphone
socket and the ability to communicate across
temporarily suppressed music by using an
internal microphone because they felt people
would still want to share their experience.
It quickly became apparent people loved the
ability to enclose themselves solely in their own
space: apparently antisocial detachment and
disappearance into a personal wonderland was
actually the ultimate desire. The hotline button
was removed on later models. Sharing would
have to wait for a much more sophisticated
and yet fundamentally prosaic means of
swapping thoughts, gossip, likes and dislikes
and an immense amount of recycled general
knowledge and secondary, processed stockpiles
of information.)

The Walkman allowed me to take the most

up-to-date music into an area that had begun its life seventy-three years before, but which could so easily be part of the contemporary world, and now have this instantly created soundtrack of modern music. The Underground network could be continually tampered with in this way, as the constant influx of passengers influenced the space and feeling of the carriage, or the corridors with their personal purpose, the particular direction they were taking through life, where they'd come from, where they were going. New energy was constantly being added to the system, so even if mostly the platforms, trains and escalators stayed where they were when they were first built, years before, there was always change, and the outside world left its mark through people and their gestures, traces, fashions, desires and accessories, through younger people always arriving taking over from those whose Underground lifespan was done, and the changing advertising and modified design that kept track of where people and the products they bought had got to in that outside world.

71

The routes, speeds and compact nineteenth-century carriage sizes stayed the same, but the Underground moved with the times; even, in its own way, the Bakerloo kept pace. If something new and innovative turned up in the world, like a Sony Walkman, it wouldn't be very long before someone turned up holding the coolest space-age pop-culture product on the planet and sat down on a Bakerloo train stuck in its groove. One world intruded into another.

7

I can't remember what the very first cassette
was that I played on the Bakerloo Line, but
thinking about where I was and where the
music I mostly listened to was in the late 1970s,
I can take a very good guess. I'm not sure
I would have made a conscious and indeed
self-conscious decision about what I was going
to play on this journey that would in its own
way be historical, recorded in the future as a
key moment in time, or if I was limited to what
I owned on cassette, or what I had recorded on
to cassette.

Whilst working at the *New Musical Express*,

I would have recorded all my interviews on a C90 cassette, forty-five minutes a side, needing a little concentration during the interview to remember to turn it over, and not lose precious words. I mostly used the same cassette, to save money, bought at Boots the Chemist, where they were cheapest, so that one week's interview with say Mick Jagger would have been taped over for next week's interview with say the somewhat less famed Monochrome Set who would then be replaced by Squeeze who were then wiped out by Robert Smith of the Cure who got talked over by Ted Nugent. On the Bakerloo, it could have been an interview I was listening to on my astounding new Walkman, with John Cooper Clarke or Gary Numan, but it probably wasn't, because I hated the sound of my own voice – even when punkishly, pompously telling Mick Jagger off for being too old, at thirty-seven, to be singing pop, I sounded like I was still helplessly stuck in Stockport, as if struck off from all action, merely fantasizing I was actually in a room with Jagger himself, attempting to organize his affairs.

It could have been something released in 1979 that was already not only my favourite album of the year but of all time, because this was – if you were approaching music from the point of view of someone my age, with my interests, my levels of anxiety and ardour, with my job on the *New Musical Express*, close to the centre of the universe, where the young assume they are, because they are right, if wrong, keen on the presence of surprise, militantly opposed to the elimination of possibilities – a year of considerable transition and purification. Elsewhere, and perhaps this new music abstractly, nervously diagnosed this, the once promising countercultural energy of the 1960s had dissipated, and a conservative countercultural revolution was looming, leading to the emergence, along the tracks, around the corner, through the next tunnel, of the controlling, fanatically moralistic New Right of Margaret Thatcher and Ronald Reagan.

This keyed-up, highly charged pre-digital new music also anticipated a world that was about to be cut into gleaming pieces by technology, television, ideology, assisted by its fancy pleasure-seeking slave, the music video, which, what with one thing and another, through roaring tunnels that stretched back to the invention of the telephone, and forward to the introduction of the Sony Walkman, eventually led to the all-change free-for-all of Facebook and Twitter. (Even as technology seemed to permit a greater appreciation of world events, greater access to obscure, enlightened activity, and open the way to transcendent global consciousness, critical standards, utopian spirit and attention spans were disintegrating to comply with the hyper-cautious, self-protecting commercial interests of those competing for customers. Possibly frightening, excessive and subversive novelty was reduced to comfortable, accessible, even consoling excitement.)

In 1979 – before this post-internet vortex of pressure and pleasure, where more and more music entertainment emerged, swept along by technology and the media-fuelled desires of listeners – certain currents and principles had made the disruptive, avant-garde end of rock music particularly engaging. There was still such an almost chaste belief in progress, a natural craving for a violent renewal of meanings, and a treatment of influences that was midway between the reverential and the murderous. It was a culmination, rearrangement, refinement of experimental ideas, sounds and principles instigated by punk. This music was labelled, possibly first of all by me, in the *NME* (perhaps thought up whilst daydreaming on the Bakerloo Line stuck outside Oxford Circus), 'post-punk'. This name, another slice of convenient collective identification, introduced to diagnose, even conceive, an apparent important cultural movement, slid into general use quite nicely, but didn't come close to expressing the concern this music and these musicians, often haunted by dread, had with spatial and rhythmic, temporal and geographical displacement, with plotting the physical universe and the individual's place in it. In some ways they were producing in advance a soundtrack to the disorientating, paradoxically lonely effect of constant contact with the internet.

Thirty-plus years after this post-punk peak, the internet with all its contributors, rituals and classifying herding systems had enabled an accelerating, fragmenting collision of timelines, fashions and eras to take place, a muddying of historical direction, a concurrent multiplication of signals, an increasing clamour for instant feedback and response, a sterile and perversely inhibiting calculation of people's tastes. Society itself was becoming a stream of consciousness, reality an object we could move around from several simultaneous perspectives with a cubist rapport or mere lust for surprise – but 1979 was still generally stuck or forced to stay stuck in the assumption that ideas and intentions marched forward and travelled in one direction, from tunnel to tunnel, platform to platform, station to station, line to line, movement to movement, genre to genre, trend to trend, modernism to post-modernism, intrepid, messy underground to commercial, regulated surface. At the time, though, because of this intact faith in the value of progress, there was a sense that music could be a response to the insidious elements of cultural orthodoxy, produced by musicians aware of the dangers that new environments presented to human sensibility, using art to detect and correct sensory bias and derangement. For post-punk activists, music wasn't meant to merely fill to bursting point machines and gadgets and players and intangible storage systems.

This 1979 music, which suggests what could have been on the first cassette I played on the Bakerloo, not heard much on Radio 1 outside of the John Peel show, where it starred, music which followed on quite naturally from music the year before, and would logically move into the 1980s, losing some of its momentum once compact discs arrived, included: *Unknown Pleasures* by Joy Division, *Entertainment!* by Gang of Four, *Metal Box* by Public Image Limited, *The Raincoats* by the Raincoats, *154* by Wire, *Lodger* by David Bowie, *Reproduction* by the Human League, *Drums and Wires* by XTC, *Cut* by the Slits, *New Picnic Time* by Pere Ubu, *A Trip to Marineville* by Swell Maps, *Dragnet* and *Live at the Witch Trials* by the Fall, *Fear of Music* by Talking Heads, *Half Machine Lip Moves* by Chrome, *Eskimo* by the Residents, *The B-52s* by The B-52s, *Y* by the Pop Group, *20 Jazz Funk Greats* by Throbbing Gristle, *This Heat* by This Heat, *Solid State Survivor* by Yellow Magic Orchestra, *pragVEC* by pragVEC, *Join Hands* by Siouxsie and the Banshees, *Mix-Up* by Cabaret Voltaire.

This arousing, prognostic network of post-punk records was indeed an underground, requiring a map to locate and decode what you perhaps needed a map to find – above ground, in bright, well-publicized spaces, at number one in the sociable charts, there was the Village People, the Bee Gees, Art Garfunkel, Cliff Richard, Dr Hook, Pink Floyd, and the only number-one songs hinting that there was this co-existing underground, perhaps forming the escalators, the stairs, between one level and another, were by Ian Dury, Blondie, the Boomtown Rats, the Police, Gary Numan and the Buggles, exuberantly designed, confident and articulate new-wave novelty songs with more of a desire to flee into the past, or perhaps a future nostalgically located in the past, where things were familiar and safe.

I would not be listening on purpose to Rod Stewart, the Eagles, Styx or Foreigner, because they seemed blasé and instantly antique, working on behalf of a mega-corporate entertainment state, with no statements to make about the future. I kept my distance from the Jam, if only because rumour had it one of them voted Tory, and they dressed as though they all did, as if punk were routine show business, a mere day job. Although I would have been paying constant close attention to Neil Young and Bob Dylan, who released *Rust Never Sleeps* and *Slow Train Coming* that year, these don't seem likely candidates for that first Walkman trip. I would have been instinctively drawn to something that belonged on this pioneering new machine that had the capacity to turn an everyday journey on the Bakerloo into an explicit plunge down the rabbit hole or tumble through the looking glass.

Other recent Bowie albums would have been appropriate – the so-called Berlin Trilogy beginning with *Low* and *Heroes* in 1977 that *Lodger* completed, so that it connected with by then contemporary groups like Joy Division who had recalibrated from their northern base much of the insidious chilled passion of Bowie's self-invented, almost Borgesian version of Berlin, transforming uncertainty into artistic energy, and the shattered, eerie post-industrial glamour of *Station to Station*, released in 1976, a parable of disorientation, an anxious journey across sinking surfaces through shadowy territory on a dangerous quest to get some bearings, which is perhaps so obvious a choice it's too obvious.

The experimental pop musician and avid explorer of hidden worlds, Brian Eno, had collaborated with Bowie on his estranged, sanctuary-seeking Berlin Trilogy, or triptych, proposing that Bowie made them, the most challenging records of his career, as a way of keeping his music fresh and 'ducking the momentum of a successful career'. There were Eno albums I could have played, some more active, frisky and louder than others, some distilling techniques, processes and philosophies of previous musical explorers Erik Satie, John Cage and Steve Reich, with their own distilling and realignment of Claude Debussy, Edgard Varese and John Coltrane, into a contemplative genre that Eno himself would gravely christen 'ambient'. These albums would have been perfect to hear under the skin through feather-light headphones to alter, adjust and intensify the experience of being on a crammed, busy or illuminated, totally empty Underground train, where sound made in the image of something as natural as the wind blowing leaves could infiltrate this allegedly secure but synthesized underworld.

A 1975 Eno album called *Discreet Music* of sculpted, formless tones drifting to and from

the edge of silence was as uncluttered as Harry
Beck's stabilizing, schematic Tube map first
proposed for the then eight lines in 1933 and
updated when necessary. His map dragged the
nineteenth-century Underground well and truly
into the twentieth century, pragmatically and
loftily outlining routes, methods, digressions
and connections that would make it all the way
through to the twenty-first century without
becoming passé, apparently quite capable
of looking poised and contemporary in the
twenty-second century. He transferred the
idea of the industrial Underground into a
timeless, streamlined concept with a definite
image. *Discreet Music* and Beck's map of the
Underground both eliminated unnecessary,
distracting material, ejected literal connectives,
and extraordinarily organized carefully selected,
ordinary material into a new reality that was
simultaneously diminished and enriched.

Beck's virtuoso geometrical map and Eno's
sensuous, unemphatic music did not move in
one direction – they moved in all directions at

once, like time does throughout the universe. Eno produced this music using electronics in the recording studio best utilized by intuitive pop musicians rather than oddly unconvinced classical musicians who had failed to see the studio as a way of refining and completing – sometimes ever beginning – their compositions: he recorded and reproduced with technological sophistication conceptual music inspired by the idea that music was organized sound instead of sanctified and regimented notes. Eno produced texturally minimal, repetitive drones with the forensic care a pop producer would apply to building a deft, rhapsodic wall of sound.

Another Eno album, 1978's faux-therapeutic *Music for Airports*, poised midway between watery muzak and a spine-tingling awakening of consciousness, contained a caressing, cascading series of voiceless, edgeless, breezeless atmospheres notionally conceived to be used in and around airports to relax tense airline passengers preparing to fly, and remind the listener of how deeply thoughtful someone must be to be truly relaxed. It would have transferred well into a displaced, low-level Tube setting, amidst all those sleek surfaces and uncanny, unknowable aromas. Liquid intelligence, textured emotion and profound prettiness would have flowed around and through me, blocking out all other booming, rattling, screeching Tube noise in the way Beck's map of the Underground had radically blocked out visual noise and irrelevant information, whilst other passengers, uneasy in their own skin, warily glanced at me from the corner of their eyes, monitoring the potentially disruptive level of my eccentricity. Was I in a possibly contented trance, or suffering from some sort of obscure perhaps contagious brain damage that required the wearing of a head contraption which resembled headphones from space?

Other music that it could have been, the music from the past I tended to play the most at that time – all albums by the Velvet Underground, the spaced-out, splintered Englishness of pre *Dark Side of the Moon* Pink

Floyd, the telepathic, serenely abstracted post-rock jazz of Miles Davis's *On the Corner*, *In a Silent Way*, *Bitches Brew*, most Hendrix, Robert Wyatt, Stooges, Joni Mitchell, John Martyn and even – in a spirit of a nerdy need for otherness, or a need to know something other than what the outside world gave and told me – the new forms, and related protean formlessness, of Tony Conrad and Faust, La Monte Young and Karlheinz Stockhausen – whose sparse, spectral 1956 electronic composition *Gesang der Jünglinge*, incorporating synthesized and natural voices (a boy soprano singing a prayer processed to seem electronic, electronic noises manipulated to seem natural), sounded like music emerging in the dead of night from Tube tunnels that connected the Bakerloo Line with underground cave cities on Jupiter. Fifty-five years later, when most forms of what was once unfamiliar, alienating electronic music had become familiar, even part of the bloodstream of the non-stop gaudy mainstream, a formulaic component in all the manufactured happiness, it would still sound like music you thought you'd dreamt; actually, it sounded like it would be what the internet dreamt about when it finally got some sleep, having convinced us that everything is everywhere and anything is everything.

Perhaps I gravitated to this harsh, or ghostly, or discordant, or narcotically static, or monstrously detached and even unrealistic music because it was my job; perhaps because it was a way of helping me work out how the mind worked, how outsiders with unhemmed spirit found satisfying places to inhabit in unsympathetic, wider society; perhaps because I wanted to show off, which in fact goes back to the job I did – but I was the kind of enthusiastic, perhaps aimless person who either wanted music to be so obscure I was out on my own working out what it meant – as if I too were adventuring and experimenting, right at the centre of important activity, feeling the glow as though it was something to do with me. If the music I liked was more popular, I wanted to think that I was the only person who really understood it, as if it had been specially made to my own specifications. The specialness was important, and I didn't want this spoilt by the thought I was sharing it with millions of others, diluting its private power, its sense of guidance and understanding.

All this music that I could have played for the very first time underground on my Walkman, whether right there from 1979 or from earlier – and indeed later (A Certain Ratio, John Foxx, the Au Pairs, Byrne and Eno's *My Life in the Bush of Ghosts*, Section 25, Sonic Youth, the Jesus and Mary Chain, Talk Talk, David Sylvian, Stone Roses, 808 State, Tortoise, Radiohead, Stereolab, Pavement, the Orb, KLF, Björk, Aphex Twin, Autechre, pole, UNKLE, Coil, Flaming Lips, the Good, the Bad and the Queen, Matmos, Mars Volta, Ricardo Villalobos, Isolée, Fourtet, Fennesz, Animal Collective, Actress, Max Richter, Sun O))) and Boris, Burial, Pantha du Prince, Laurel Halo, Julia Holter) – was sound that would have directly or indirectly influenced or been directly or indirectly influenced by a group formed in Germany in 1968 called Can.

Their name could represent a sealed container, a handy small vessel for holding food and drink; or it was a verb suggesting being able to do things, to do anything, to have the power and skill to move anywhere in any direction as far as possible. It was a word, and a word itself is a container, for something that held various substances; and a word for something that made things happen. Can is also short for cannabis, which is a drug that brought to the surface creative ideas in subconscious development whether they are ready or not. Bakerloo brown was hashish brown.

Can were less a rock group than a compact orchestra, a jazz collective, a cartel of dreamers, a loose affiliation of individuals, a battery of technicians, a faction of dissidents, a circle of minds, a square of mystics, a haze of weed, an ambush of gurus, a buccaneer of savants, a warp of collaborators, a cabal of freaks, a body of procedures, a lightness of heads, an education of vagabonds. By the time they made three nonchalantly mesmerizing albums called *Tago Mago*, *Ege Bamyasi* and *Future Days* between 1971 and 1973 that sounded like a heady fusion of nothing on earth, the mysterious noise of nature, a longing for something that was missing, and a different memory they were each having of the same thing, their line-up was: Holgar Czukay (bass), Irmin Schmidt (piano/organ), both students of Stockhausen; Jake Liebezeit (percussion); Michael Karoli (guitar), a student of Czukay, a decade younger than the others; and Damo Suzuki (vocals).

Suzuki had been found as a sort of preaching busker singing or praying in the streets of Munich for money and didn't so much sing as chant words or syllables as though he'd forgotten how to speak, or never could, or was inventing a new language that only he understood. He managed to do this as though he was a storyteller, navigating us through new, slightly fiendish experiences, and Johnny Rotten had certainly listened to him a lot so that his Public Image group sounded crudely speaking like the Sex Pistols influenced by Can suspended in space.

Karoli played guitar as though the source for rock was not the blues but electricity itself, breathing, and X-rays. Once he got going, sorting out the radiant pulse and general spatial blending, Liebezeit drummed up melodious, insomniac rhythms as though he'd better not stop or the world would stop. Schmidt played keyboards like he was inventing an amazing new musical instrument as he went along. Czukay played the bass like it was a living creature he loved but slightly feared. They made up compositions, sounding like they were following John Cage's prudent advice to avoid creative paralysis by 'beginning anywhere', producing sound that was inspired by Stockhausen, Eastern rhythms, free jazz, process experiments, Dada-esque happenings, a tolerance for ambiguities, Zen thought, obscure folk, imaginary cultures, cosmic utopianism and the disturbed, sensationally cogent New York art pop of the Velvet Underground.

It was music made by people who loved the thought of music where you did not know if you were actually hearing it or only imagining that you were. If there was a list of how Can could be labelled, which contained about thirty or forty possibilities for describing the music they made and the way it tripped and spiralled out of radio interference as much as James Brown, Sun Ra, Xenakis, Lee 'Scratch' Perry, John Lee Hooker, Grateful Dead, Terry Riley, Japanese Noh Theatre and Ornette Coleman, then 'rock group' was well down that list.

As was 'krautrock', the convenient collective name given in a slightly jokey, slightly wary and affectionately patronizing way to an eclectic collection of radicalized German groups from very different parts of the country that contained musicians who were born in the few years before, during or just after the Second World War. Another collective name for these groups, still frivolous but more descriptive of their mission to create sound never heard before on our planet, and invent music that could make you feel you were leaving the Earth behind, was '*kosmische*'. As well as Can, these groups included Kraftwerk, Tangerine Dream, Amon Duul II, Cluster, Popol Vuh, Harmonia, Neu! and Faust, and they were looking for ways to repair their traumatic recent history, remove the crippling infection of fascism, break free of totalitarian artistic repression, negotiate turbulent social and emotional currents, and radically, romantically reinstate the positive, progressive elements of their mortified national psyche.

They probably couldn't agree on anything, apart from the fact they didn't agree on anything, united only by vaguely parallel philosophical objectives; and they were bracketed together mainly because of the national history and context, and the links between them because of the nature of their experiments with music, performance and electronics – where they worked like painters who had eliminated paint, replacing it with sound and noise. Also linking them, perhaps, was the spectre, the awareness, the modulated, post-linear cosmos of Karlheinz Stockhausen, a notorious, internationally known techno-shaman from within their corrupted land who emerged from deeper inside the grim Nazi shadow (he was seventeen when the war ended) with a clear, spiritualized vision – an act of revenge – of how to morally and politically break free of the poisoned past and dream up the future and a new sort of other-worldly national sensibility. Having witnessed how the Nazis had turned art into an eviscerated form of controlling propaganda, he was devoted – with audacious, transcendent innocence, at the opposite extreme of fascism – to opening minds, possibilities, cultural and national borders, to regaining a mythical understanding of the world. 'The cities have been razed,' he said, 'and we can start again from the ground up without regard for the ruins and relics of a time "without taste".' For some, the forbidding concrete music of Stockhausen was as ugly, antagonistic and disconnected as the concrete, rubble-clearing modernist architecture that was hastily constructed to remove a ruined past, taking with it history, tradition and familiar focal points, as if everything from the past was to blame for the Third Reich. For others, he was a new beginning after the post-war hell, necessarily, ferociously futuristic in order to remake pulverized history and reanimate the beauty that is linked to but not overwhelmed by history.

Out of a syndicate of disciples and protégés keen on following no one, but following the vaporous flag of Stockhausen, his politics of the imagination, his avoidance of a specific political agenda – who were also inspired, directly or indirectly, by visceral philosopher and conceptual artist Joseph Beuys's messianic, strategic methods of reviving Germany's spiritual energy – a certain history can be told about a number of groups, essentially conceptual projects packaged and presented as rock artefacts, who have ended up becoming some of the most important and influential of rock groups whether they intended that or not. From Kraftwerk, Can, Neu! and Faust, speculative, observational artists creating their work in a recording studio with what could be called a post-Impressionist, even cubist approach, came a way of electronically manipulating, treating and structuring sound, establishing rhythm, heightening dramatic effect and capturing experience that significantly extended the structural and sonic possibilities of all forms of pop and rock music from the commercial to the extreme.

These musicians were fascinated by weirder, wilder alternative Anglo-American pop music, made by people their age, embedded in their own troubled history, craving their own brand of freedom. They treated this prolific, volatile pop music as an abstract framework inside which to place their more radical, probing and intellectually challenging ideas about sound, politics, art and history. Needing so much to invent new cultural space, a whole new revitalized identity, after the catastrophe of fascism, they were deeply attuned to avoiding the numbing force of cliché, including the new clichés and habits of rock, which had an imperialist, conquering edge, already something predictable and worryingly privileged in terms of their limited and limiting influences.

These new German musicians were to some extent making a new classical music following on from savage, edited *musique concrète* and tonally opulent, romantically influenced minimalism, experimenting with tape-recording techniques and multi-track recording that prefigured sampling and remixing, but hearing provocative ideas at the more experimental end of rock and the more electronic end of pop; this led to them placing a repetitive groove resembling a funk groove, a psychedelic rock groove, even a compelling disco groove, inside lengthy abstract compositions that seemed to be pondering the shape of the solar system, the colour of orgasm and the density of experience. Pinning a consoling, pleasing, almost jocular rhythm within epochal, Stockhausen-inspired pools and patterns

of sound and noise rotating past each other
with random, tingling electro-acoustic precision
meant that in 1976, before all that 1979 post-
punk commotion which connected a lot of the
dots Can helped scatter into the universe, Can
had a minor hit. They crept on to *Top of the Pops*
miming to the Dali disco of 'I Want More' as
an unholy one-hit wonder, a libertine novelty
act, muted maniacs, prophets dressed as tramps,
treated as curios, spooks out of their skulls
possibly needing to be exorcized by nervous non-
believers before they caused a change in human
behaviour. This was my kind of pop group.

8

In the same way that I cannot exactly remember the first time I travelled on the Tube, or what the first piece of music was I played underground on my Walkman, I cannot remember the first search I made on Google. One day it wasn't there, the next day it was, and very soon it was like it had always been a part of life, possibly because what you searched for on it had always been there. You hadn't known how to get there, though, and if you did know, you really didn't have the time. Now, Google gave you time, and time became something else.

I started using Google in 1997, because that

is when I got my first computer, but the first search is lost in the time that is now not what it was – I must have been so excited I immediately forgot the details, and cannot even recall how rough and ready the very first search may or may not have been or if I found what I was looking for. I have now got used to Googling the way I got used to travelling on the Tube, and have long left behind the sense of astonishment that I can use it to go anywhere to anyone at a moment's notice with limited fuss.

Google representing the internet approximates the same relation to reality as the London Underground does to London itself. The internet is a distorted, distorting and glowing reflection of a more solid, complex reality, a representation of how you can move across and inside reality, where it comes to an end, where it is most chaotic and overpopulated, where it runs out of meaning, where it is nothing but a prejudiced, almost censoring compilation of organized information selected in order to coordinate and confirm the version of reality that has been collectively decided upon.

It is in the same place as everyday life and yet in another place, which we slip into in much the same way we slip from above to below when we use the Tube. It is another space and yet *in* another space, where we are still ourselves, but not what we are when we are outside it. At some point Google changed human behaviour, and one way you can check when that moment might be is to Google it by putting something in the search box that will set you off on a journey towards the destination of knowing something new. Your answers might explain how Google has become all at once the stage, the media, the entertainer, the performance, the tradition, the artist breaking free of tradition, the glamour, the information, the shop, the consumer, the lecturer, the pupil, the architect, the illusion, the future, in the way of future, the concept conceptualizing itself, the end of progress, an early-warning system, extreme proof of compulsive collector and sculptor

Joseph Cornell's statement that collage equals reality, and around the edges the beginning of a new form of government; or it is simply a convenient way of informing you about delays on the Bakerloo Line and finding a recipe for vegetable lasagne.

Googling immediately became a daily occurrence, easily an intoxicating habit. As soon as I do anything now that concerns events and details from the old reality it leads to a Google search, to see where reality has rested, and changed shape, and been turned into a degraded or demented, spoilt or special version of the original, and how as a constantly adapting series of distractions, instructions and directions it moves towards being something that could eventually be more dominant and regulated than pre-internet reality. Already, traditional solid reality starts to look less and less real, as our mind gets infected and dislodged by virtual images of reality. The more we can monitor the world, and its shadow domains, its sweeping nature, the more we are monitored.

The world started to Google itself.

Inevitably, like I was breathing, once writing this book, finding a way to begin, I researched through Google the Bakerloo Line and any connections with music, which led to four findings, each of which could provide a history of music, abandoned or still travelling. You can make of this information what you want – like the Tube, Google will take you where you want to go, within its reach, and then what you do when you get there is up to you. You can make something happen, or let things happen to you, or go back to where you were, and start all over again.

There was a piece by hard swing jazz trumpeter Kenny Baker, his signature tune, the brash, confident 'Bakerloo Non-Stop', released as the 45 rpm B-side to 'Trumpet Blues and Cantabile' in 1958. Baker was one of the very few British jazz musicians from the 1940s and 1950s with an international reputation – part of the formidable Ted Heath dance band for three years after the war, and then leader of a number of his own groups including Baker's Dozen and his Half Dozen, a member of other bands and a well-used session musician. His music was released on the small, independent Nixa label, founded in 1950, bought by TV and radio manufacturers Pye in 1953, the second label after Decca to release albums.

Nixa, whose biggest act was the engaging singer and actress Petula Clark, supplies a history of pleasant, pre-rock and roll, pre-Beatles pop music, when music for the young was predominantly mild and well mannered, before music became the way young people self-confidently organized their lives, their personalities, their whole spinning position on the planet. You can see how far music travelled inside ten years the other side of the Beatles from Baker by looking at a skinhead ska group called the Pyramids, influenced by Prince Buster and Sam and Dave, who had a minor hit in 1969 with 'All Change for the Bakerloo Line', and a Cream/Hendrix-influenced heavy rock blues trio actually called Bakerloo, who supported the early Led Zeppelin on their Marquee debut on 18 October 1968. They were originally called the Bakerloo Blues Band, formed in Birmingham in 1968, briefly championed by John Peel; but I have no recollection of them at all, even though I once owned an album they appeared on.

This wasn't their one and only album, their self-titled debut was released in December 1969, but it was released on Harvest, EMI's in-house version of an underground, progressive rock label like Island Records or Track, to compete with the similarly devised Deram of staid Decca, and Vertigo of even more staid Philips. These labels created the template on which Richard Branson's Virgin label would be based in 1972 by his music-fan sidekick Simon Draper. In those days labels released cheap less-than-half-full-priced sampler albums containing a showcase collection of their acts so that poor music fans like me, only able to afford an album every month or so, could try out some of their more experimental acts that you'd read about in the *New Musical Express* but might miss on the John Peel show.

In 1971, the year the United Kingdom decimalized its currency, I bought a second-hand copy for 75 pence – 15 shillings – of a double album Harvest sampler released the year before at the full price of 29*s*. 11*d*. (roughly £1.50) called *Picnic – A Breath of Fresh Air*. It featured the then famous Deep Purple, Pink Floyd and the Pretty Things, as well as the label's more obscure acts needing promotion, and it's how I found out at the age of fourteen about four of my all-time favourite musicians, Roy Harper, Kevin Ayers, Syd Barrett and Michael Chapman. Bakerloo were on the sampler but might as well have been lost in the post.

I have found that I can write thousands of words about the music I like. The music I don't like comes down to almost nothing but the facts, there isn't much more to say – and the facts were Led Zeppelin became superstars, Bakerloo split up after a year, members went on to work with Coliseum, Uriah Heep and

Humble Pie, disappearing from view until the internet found them, and repeated the bare facts. I could write about Bakerloo the group for five minutes; conclude that their blues was fairly brown, and note that of all the things produced by their producer, Gus Dudgeon, including David Bowie's 'Space Oddity', early Elton John, the Bonzo Dog Doo-Dah Band and an early example of sampling, a tape loop of tribal drumming at the heart of John Kongos's 1971 'He's Gonna Step On You Again', Bakerloo was the most forgotten.

I have been writing about Can one way or another for thirty-five years, because the facts are the beginning of the story, not the end, and their blues burst with the blueness of sea, space, sky and spirit, their blues are so blue they are the colour of everything as it pops up out of the blue, the blue in the distance that Leonardo da Vinci said to capture on a canvas you must make five times bluer. As magically blue and elsewhere as Can were, they found their way to the vicinity of the brown Bakerloo Line.

Can's 'Up the Bakerloo with Anne' was recorded in the BBC's Maida Vale studio complex along the Delaware Road, built as an ice rink in 1909, home of the BBC Symphony Orchestra from 1934, and the standby centre for their news service during the Second World War. The Radiophonic Workshop was created and based there from 1958, a warren of rooms at street level spanning a very long corridor. Inspired by what had been happening in experimental French broadcasting, it was a research-and-development lab for exploring electronic sound and generating original sound effects, mostly used for writing signature tunes, jingles and background scores for radio and television programmes. Most famously, in 1963, at a time when the world appeared threatened with imminent atomic destruction, and the Beatles were suggesting an alternative, the workshop was responsible for the pre-synthesizer synthetic *Dr Who* theme tune, part oscillating *musique concrète*, part honeyed light melodic, which implied the Doctor was from the same planet as Stockhausen but also James Last. Under the supervision of Brian Hodgson, the workshop also crafted the time-travelling take-off and landing sound for the Doctor's Tardis time machine, fabricating an antique modern noise that appropriately seemed to be travelling in two directions at once. Inside rooms tucked a level or two under the ground, the Maida Vale Studios is where most of the John Peel sessions by old and new Peel favourites were recorded, to avoid the problem that there was only a limited amount of commercially recorded music allowed on the radio.

Because of various commercial and union rules, the BBC was tightly restricted when it came to the amount of records it could play each day. The pioneering commercial radio station Radio Luxembourg, which had shrewdly targeted the swarming new teenage pop fans since the early 1960s, was free of British legal restrictions and able to play pop music more or less non-stop between 6 p.m. and 2 a.m.

Every Sunday between 11 p.m. and midnight all through the 1960s it would play that week's Top 20 in tense, unpredictable reverse order. This made the charts seem particularly exotic and intoxicating to those of us smuggling a transistor radio into bed without our parents' knowledge, setting off for school the next day with some sort of phosphorescent, forbidden knowledge transmitted seemingly from outer space about pop songs and pop singers ringing through our minds having ambushed our dreams. This feeling was a spectacular antidote to classic youthful insecurity. The nation's fascination with pop music can perhaps be traced back to how the pop charts first solidified in many people's minds, as something forcing its spellbinding, constantly changing ways through sizzling static interference and the tipsy warping of failing batteries into the ears and the enclosed, erotically charged private bed space of youngsters anxiously staying awake much later than they were allowed.

Unlicensed, pirate radio stations such as

Caroline, moored beyond national boundaries and therefore devilishly free of formal broadcasting requirements and the record company control of Radio Luxembourg, were able to extend this idea of non-stop pop music into daytime hours. It was irresistible, it's what 1960s listeners were impatiently waiting for, an unfettered access to pop songs. The BBC was forced to catch up, or die, and within three years of the 1964 launch of Radio Caroline they had sensibly organized their response. Despite the conditions that still existed about how much vinyl they could actually play, Radio 1 was their slightly square, cock-eyed version of the dynamic, music-loving, fashionable, risky-seeming now-ness of the pirate radio stations. Radio 1 played pop music during the day, the music getting stranger, or stronger, as it passed into the evening towards the end-of-night John Peel show. Things, for better or worse, would never be the same again.

One way round the 'needle time' rules and regulations about how many records Radio

I could play during the day was to have groups play sessions recorded in the BBC's own recording studio – BBC radio could play these tracks recorded in-house, and were not therefore playing records. This set up another world where bands created shadow versions of their repertoire – spare, mercurial versions that were in some new zone between transitory live performances and fixed recorded artefacts.

It was a weird meeting of experimental young radicalism and the BBC as an organization doing its best for an abstract idea of the population based on idealistic principles established in the 1930s by remote, discriminating minds committed to ensuring a mythical, mind-improving quality of life. It was a unique coalition of impassive, thorough bureaucracy working under the most eccentrically established technological and administrative limitations and the unlimited minds of young musicians suddenly finding the freedom to make up their own rules. It was a different kind of tension from the one worked out between expression and commerce in the record industry, one between romantic artists and scientific business minds, but it produced similar effects. The BBC, known very much then as Auntie, was the cautious, fastidious, curiously generous protector of the nation's apparent best interests. Somehow, this involved allowing John Peel to operate freely, if stashed away in an alternative zone. Because of the quantity of Peel sessions, and the perceptive choices, this means many of the most fascinating and innovative groups of the last fifty years, including all of those 1979 post-punk groups, were caught in the surreptitious other world of Peel.

The Peel sessions, effectively curated by Peel and his long-time producer John Walters, are another example of one reality shadowing another, connected to the conventional recorded history of music like the Underground is to the city above – it's another version of a musical system, corresponding to the more known one, but existing elsewhere, out of view, needing a certain knowledge to navigate. The collected Peel sessions can take you through the history of British rock music, but because these sessions were recorded quickly on more primitive equipment, under less commercial, almost laboratory conditions, with an anonymous in-house BBC producer, there is a difference in tone and approach. The sessions become a plan, a hint of yet another world mapped out in relation to, but distant from, this one, existing below the surface. The history of popular music as defined by the Peel sessions of hundreds and hundreds of groups, from the smallest to the biggest, the most obscure to the most iconic, recorded between 1967 and 2004.

Bands who recorded at Maida Vale would report how it was like stepping back into the past, into an abandoned-seeming world where the staff wore ties and brown coats, the equipment seemed built during the war to spy on the Germans, and switches and buttons were operated by Bakelite knobs and aeroplane joysticks. The engineers at Maida

Vale, part of a BBC that was itself consumed in rituals less sober and censoring than the establishment BBC, loved this sort of technical challenge – how to make a group sound as original, as epic and intimate as they wanted, whilst recording four tracks in a day, using old-fashioned equipment, and probably making music that was not as such their cup of tea whilst drinking cups of tea. Workers inside the great controlling machinery of the BBC have their own experimental urges, and work for the company because it seems to be a place that, in its own eccentric way, in out-of-the-way buildings and rooms, removed from the more fixed Broadcasting House, finds ways to encourage the pioneering and the inspired.

The nearest Tube to this independent-minded outpost of the BBC is Maida Vale on the Bakerloo Line, seven stops from Oxford Circus. When Peel came to name an unrelated track without a formal title from a Can album session that was recorded at Maida Vale in February 1973, he turned the problem into a competition, and asked his listeners for their suggestions. It's not clear how many people actually replied, but out of the entries, Peel chose the title 'Up the Bakerloo with Anne', Anne being Annie Nightingale, Radio 1's first ever female disc jockey, for years the only one, whose own tastes veered more towards night-time Peel than daytime jaunty.

Peel's cheeky choice for the title was Peel being Peel, deflecting attention away from whatever he was up to that might be considered by the powers that be subversive by adopting a slightly puckish, comic and therefore unthreatening persona, as though the obnoxious, clannish sexism makes him like other 'loveable' Radio 1 disc jockeys, one of the boys, up for a (surely harmless) laugh. In the same way therefore that Can were krautrock, conveniently, safely pinned down into a flip, almost camp category, this track, what Can called a spontaneous composition, the purest, improvising side of the group where they joined with the impromptu self-expression of jazz, without the subsequent editing, splicing and manipulating, was titled outside the group, referring to the brown colour of the Bakerloo. This brown, a bit smutty, is another reason why the image of Bakerloo suffers from its given colour.

Peel's chosen title for the Can track was a sniggering, boorish reference to anal intercourse, 'up the Bakerloo' being a slang term like 'Marmite motorway' or 'Bourneville boulevard', but it didn't get close to explicitly noting what was truly transgressive and transporting about Can. John Peel was always in whimsical disguise, as if he never wanted it to be known that what he played could actually change human behaviour, certainly not inside the BBC where he acted like a droll, off-beat uncle wearing crumpled brown and smoking a pipe, harmlessly and endlessly tinkering with the weirdest, ugliest sort of music, like it was a greasy, worn-out old engine that would never work again. (Forty years after the track got its title, I asked Annie Nightingale, the longest-serving Radio 1 broadcaster following Peel's death in 2004, if she knew about the Can track and its title. Nikki Sudden of Swell Maps, an experimental montage-pop imagining of what Can would sound like influenced by T. Rex, had told her, twenty years later. Peel and Annie were the only BBC DJs to play Swell Maps. Until then, she hadn't known. 'It took years and years for me to find out. I think the title was taking the piss a bit,' she shrugged, 'but I still think it's quite an honour, having a track by such a fantastic group named after me.' She now lives in Maida Vale. 'So the Bakerloo is my favourite line.')

The Bakerloo piece is Can at their best, when they had got to know each other so well, in the middle of making their best music, beginning, without warning, out of nowhere, out of the ground, from the sky, the clock is ticking, time is fixed, their minds are ticking over, constant pondering, time is molten, the five of them travelling in the same direction, but on different routes, never leaving each other alone. It lasts about as long as it would take to get from Baker

Street to the northern outpost of the line –
about thirty-five minutes.

Music by Can could sound like a Tube
journey, the sound of this other city making its
constant move from light to dark to light, danger
to safety, people in people out, so Peel wasn't
simply smirking, being completely disingenuous,
when he titled the homeless Can session 'Up the
Bakerloo': each line with its own distinct rattles,
thumps and murmurs, each station approached
and left behind with a distinct clicking, clattering
rhythm, whirring motors, each tunnel a sound
world of its own, the noise of the machinery,
elevators rolling, lifts descending, trains surging,
metal scraping, doors electronically opening
and closing, footsteps drumming, headphones
leaking, wheels pulsating, carriages shuddering,
tantalizing snatches of overheard conversation,
pages turning, whispers of desire, random
squeaks, intestinal churn, clangs, taps and
bleeps, menacing information transmitted over
loudspeakers sparkling with static, sampled,
computer-generated voices, warning, guiding,

repeating, the next station will be, the sudden
silences, the accidental edits, segues and
scratches between one sound and another,
the accumulating tension, the vacillating
combination of rhythms and densities, electronic
scatter, stationary tranquillity abruptly annexed
by indeterminate rumbles from deep below,
the sound being edited and manipulated
by how you move through it, react to it and
process it through your own experience. The
sound of a Tube journey can seem like a piece
of music, one reflecting a city in suspense,
a cluster of catacombs, set apart, on the
move, spontaneously composed, recorded
and mixed by the likes of Can, a layering of
texture, movement and rhythm, a collision of
memory and mood, a caving in of certainty,
a representation of trust.

I stopped using my Walkman after a few
months once the novelty wore off; it was already
looking out of date, in a world it helped create
that was quickly picking up speed. I preferred
the natural noises of the Underground, and

preferred listening to music in private, as though I was still under a blanket, at midnight, up to no good, listening through one ear to something gloriously different that had travelled from afar through crackles of sin, dwindling batteries and approaching dreams. The Walkman marched on in the form of newer models, different skin, flashier form, longer battery life, characterless compact discs soon replacing cassettes; and then in a world where the technology was the show business, the streamlined iPod as a more bewitching performer, a more serpentine icon, effectively replaced the Walkman, which became a period piece. By the time the iPod becomes a period piece (not long now), having comprehensively sucked with various associates the inspiring disorderliness, the obscure power, out of music, the replacement will be in control of our dreams.

9

I'd stopped working for the *NME* by 1983,
and my Bakerloo route between Baker Street
and Oxford Circus was used less and less. The
Bakerloo fell away from being a line I would
use every day as I moved around London, and
I eventually ended up, as a northerner, mostly
using the Northern Line. I would come across
the Bakerloo now and then, the way it crossed
and was crossed by the other lines; persevering,
patched up, licked with paint, re-tiled, smelling
more clearly of fabric conditioner, fast food and
deodorant, it was stuck where it was, infected by
the outside world, but minding its own business,

under orders, behaving itself, somewhere still more 1916 than 1960, and yet more 1999 than 1939, sometimes seeming a little spent and shaky, especially around monumental, mutating Paddington and shapeless Edgware Road, where it was most pounded and unloved, taken for granted, a mere workhorse, but it felt more capable and tireless as it ploughed along the surface, chasing freedom or pure timeless speed north through Willesden and the stalled hinterland beyond.

It remains the line where, a few stops either side of Baker Street, on my own, with no one else in the carriage, as the platform slips away, heading to the station where I change on to another line, another dimension, closer to home, and love, sat amidst incandescent electric light as midnight approaches, I can feel as lonely as I have ever felt, with only the fading, flickering Tube travelling traces I have left behind over the years for company, phantom set into the shuddering window opposite me, just me, moving nowhere fast, as though the light will keep getting brighter and brighter, trapped inside all that immense surrounding darkness, until there is nothing left but almighty lightness and implacable motion, a noise like the flowing of water over rocks, and a feeling that the outside world had drifted beyond my reach, into oblivion, and the next stop never arrives.

The Bakerloo bravely carries on, outlasting all the innovations, changes in fashion, new fads, new fascinations, new idols, new psychology, keeping pace with the coalescing technology that is transforming the surface world into a remote image of itself. It keeps on going, as if nothing is yet finished, and it has only been operating for a short while. It carries on being brown, humble, unloveable, what it is; but it is ultimately as mysterious, as contemporary, as dynamic a performer – on stage, expressing itself in its own way, in front of a constantly changing audience – as anything on the planet.

As long as the Bakerloo keeps going, up and down, through and around, under and under, appointment to appointment, people in people out, with their own ideas, never changing, creating rhythm, moving on, everything around it changing, noise being made, and however far into the future things go, the transformed, transforming city above and below will still rely on the Bakerloo, flat brown, cosmic brown, over a century old, which moves along the tracks through tunnel after tunnel stop after stop zone after zone through arbitrary chronological realms all the way back into the smoke of time the speed of invention the flux of memory the spinning of the Earth and all the way forward to something else we will do for the first time and not really remember, which a great piece of music, movement within space, leaps across time, one moment replaced by another, becoming the future, prepares us for . . .

The heart-stopping end of the line.

10

Can, on their way to the end of the line, and a
spiralling afterlife, increasingly acclaimed and
influential, looking like a hippy rock group, at
the edge of society, wearing brown, filed under
'krautrock', experimenting with tape collage,
acting like surrealist clowns appreciating how
nonsense can be the purest form of freedom,
sounding like travellers migrating through
the space there is between space and time,
made Can music. Can music remembered
music from the future that had not happened
yet: by remembering it, as though it was an
ordinary thing to remember the future, they

made it happen. It is a genre all of its own that ended up splitting up into so many genres and connected genres that you could use a map like Harry Beck's to explain it all.

By the end of the 1970s, towards the end of the vinyl era, as a going, composing, recording concern, as a floating line-up of ghosts, after a few more irresistible albums including *Future Days* and *Soon Over Babaluma*, models of home-made eternity, Can passed away, and there are many facts available through a basic Google search about what happened to the various members of the group, and their reputation and influence.

The facts, expressing the story mostly agreed upon, offer a superficial hint about how the music of Can, points of focus, centres of concentration, glamorous ebb and flow, saying little but singing much, creating not so much a new world but a special, alert awareness of one, settled over the history of modern music like a spreading mist. They're around more than they ever were when they were fully operating, and the 'Music of Can' was at the centre of the May 2012 I'll Be Your Mirror relative of the genre-crashing All Tomorrow's Parties series of artist-curated contemporary-music festivals held around the world. Unreleased Can music was presented almost reverently at London's Alexandra Palace, and amongst a three-day bill containing a variety of outsider acts representing where the underground has gone, shadowing the radical, making music forty years after Can, including Mogwai, Archers of Loaf, Harvey Milk, El-P, Thee Oh Sees and Forest Swords, Can still sounded as though they are always what follows.

As we move towards a stage where all the recorded music in the world that there ever was and is can be heard in one place in one room on one speaker at one time, if all that music was played at once, from the noisiest to the loveliest, from the catchiest to the smartest, from the most unhinged to the most remorseful, the angriest to the tenderest, and you could cope with working it all out as it all happened at once, then it would sound more or less exactly like Can.

Can are themselves a map, they are a complete network, the embodiment of an entire history of electronic music, the original source of which you could find in the same year that there was the first sign of the London Underground, the opening of the first Underground line between Bishops Road, Paddington and Farringdon Road, which became part of the Bakerloo. In 1863, four years before the invention of the first practical modern typewriter, the year of the birth of the Underground, the prophetic German writer, mathematician, physicist and physiologist Hermann Ludwig Ferdinand von Helmholtz, author of a book named *On the Sensations of Tone as a Physiological Basis for the Theory of Music*, built an electronically controlled resonator for studying and synthetically creating musical tones and human speech. His 'Helmholtz Resonator' demonstrated that air cavities have sonic resonance, uncovered the physical and visual properties of sound, and answered questions about why one note sounds different from another. These were the first hints of the availability of a potentially limitless new extravaganza of sounds that could be found outside conventional instruments.

His experiments were not done from a musical point of view, but they can be counted as the first button pressed, the first manufactured note produced, the first sound synthetically created, in a history of electronic music picked up by Can where Stockhausen, Varese, the BBC's Radiophonic Workshop and pioneering pop producers developing multi-track recording in the early 1960s left off. Stockhausen and Varese, the Workshop's tinkering and the pop producers' electronically generated and shaped sound had picked up from where in Paris in 1948 radio engineer Pierre Schaeffer, picking up from John Cage's 1939 *Imaginary Landscape*, composed perhaps the first piece of *musique concrète*, 'Étude aux chemins de fer', a 'concert of noises' made up entirely from the sounds of steam trains. Schaeffer in turn moved on from the first electrical recording of a symphony orchestra in 1925, Leopold Stokowski and the Philadelphia Orchestra performing Camille Saint-Saëns' 1874 *Danse Macabre* tone poem, from how Busoni, piano virtuoso successor to the visionary Liszt (b.1811), had noted at the beginning of the twentieth century that 'the full flowering of music is frustrated by our instruments, their range, their tone', and that in any great new music, machines 'would be assigned a share in it'.

On the Can map, lines criss-cross, merge and dart here, there and everywhere, some busier and more familiar than others around a central point that is itself always on the move, fanning out to the emptier edges of the map that might yet be filled in; the main lines on this Can map include trance, ambient, trip hop, electronica, dub, hip hop, world, post-rock, post-punk, drum and bass, industrial, house, techno, garage; and stops along the way include grime, dubstep, euro-trance, dream house, coldwave, electro hop, dark core, chill out, electro clash, laptronica, neurofunk, new age, dubtronica, bitpop, illbient, glitch, ambient house, euro-pop, fork gaze, sparkle prog and lowercase. So if you need to know how to find where new music has moved since Busoni's future-fancying 1906 document of intent, how to move from Morton Feldman to Gorillaz changing lines only once, from Silver Apples to Chemical Brothers a few stops across the centre, from Senking to Rihanna in four stops, from Harrison Birtwistle to Ben Frost in three, from John Cage to *Dr Who* in two, to see where music has gone since the 1960s when there was just a gentle handful of genres and most music from the Archies to Captain Beefheart was filed under 'pop', then you can begin and end with this Can map.

Oddly enough, you can begin with the Bakerloo Line, where Can found themselves, without even knowing it, because they didn't know where they were going, but knew there was a way to get there. Can, in a tightly packed can, on cassette, let's say, because it makes sense, that it was the first music I played on my Sony Walkman whilst sitting on a Bakerloo train heading to the *NME* offices reading a piece I had written about, well, Can: the thrilling inner life of their music, how they made up their own rules, for a world where you live and die by chance, even though the piece might appear to be about something else, about many other things, about how you plan a route through life, about how you work out how to belong, how you order space in order to name, speak and think, about how you get to the BBC studios near Maida Vale from the BBC studios near Oxford Circus, how you travel in just a few stops from the cracked pavements of Harlesden to the stock tourist sites scattered around Piccadilly, from one extreme of a great city's strangeness to another, about technological novelty, the twentieth-century boom in mass production, the revolution of electricity, about the emergence of new artistic forms and

languages to represent new environmental
demands, the swift acceptance of the enigma of
online activity, leading to an increasing change
in what the 'here and now' actually means,
about how you define the sensation that music
produces, and how the music you like becomes
a part of you, about how Clande Debussy
said in 1910 that the century of the aeroplane
has a right to its own music, about how the
language of Chopin turned within two hundred
years into the language of King Crimson, the
language of Wagner into the language of Daft
Punk, about a history of post-Second World
War Germany that ends with producer Konrad
'Conny' Plank working as Marlene Dietrich's
sound engineer, assisting Edgard Varese, and
going on to collaborate with Cluster, Neu!
and Kraftwerk, about how you see yourself
reflected in others, about a sense of yearning
for a future you know will never come to pass,
the unstable chemistry of cultural transmission,
about how the most significant change in art
over the past century was collage, and a word

is a word is a word is a collage, the influence on
human behaviour and culture of technicians
and mechanical engineers, the extraordinary,
hallucinatory clarity of recorded music, about
how power becomes form, the impermanence
of all things, where beauty leads to ruin, about
the spatial context for our experiences, the
tempo of capitalism, the role of observation
versus the role of the imagination, how lived
memory evolves into historical memory, about
the shadowy recesses of everyday life, about
a world constantly requiring new forms of
attention, the boundaries between outside
and inside, about Busoni's declaration that
'music was born free, and to win freedom is
its destiny', about alternative histories, about
how one colour, or one sound, or one logo can
say so much, for better or worse, about what
it feels like to do something for the first time,
about what happens to your mind when you
are sat on the Underground, in close proximity
to chaos, when you are stuck, with nothing in
your head but your memories, and memories

of memories, which form a map, some more
recent than others, some about music, which
you can almost hear, smashed into the spilling
sounds of the segmented, centre-less city
below, a vast imaginary landscape waiting to be
discovered, about how you find what you are
looking for sometimes by not directly looking at
it, not by skimming the surface, not by checking
what others have said, or cross-referencing
what the facts are, but by heading off into the
next tunnel, which curves away from now, away
from the facts, picking up speed, in the bold
direction of what happens next, a beautiful and
dangerous new world, arriving and departing
at the same time, stirring under our feet,
containing secrets, turning above our heads,
in the open air, suddenly.

PENGUIN LINES

Choose Your Journey

If you're looking for...

Romantic Encounters

Heads and Straights
by Lucy Wadham
(the Circle line)

Waterloo—City, City—Waterloo
by Leanne Shapton
(the Waterloo & City line)

Tales of Growing Up and Moving On

Heads and Straights
by Lucy Wadham
(the Circle line)

A Good Parcel of English Soil
by Richard Mabey
(the Metropolitan line)

Mind the Child
by Camila Batmanghelidjh and
Kids Company
(the Victoria line)

The 32 Stops
by Danny Dorling
(the Central line)

A History of Capitalism
According to the Jubilee Line
by John O'Farrell
(the Jubilee line)

A Northern Line Minute
by William Leith
(the Northern line)

Mind the Child
by Camila Batmanghelidjh and
Kids Company
(the Victoria line)

Heads and Straights
by Lucy Wadham
(the Circle line)

**Laughter and
Tears**

**Breaking
Boundaries**

Drift
by Philippe Parreno
(the Hammersmith & City line)

Buttoned-Up
by Fantastic Man
(the East London line)

Waterloo–City, City–Waterloo
by Leanne Shapton
(the Waterloo & City line)

Earthbound
by Paul Morley
(the Bakerloo line)

Mind the Child
by Camila Batmanghelidjh
and Kids Company
(the Victoria line)

The Blue Riband
by Peter York
(the Piccadilly line)

A Bit of Politics

The 32 Stops
by Danny Dorling
(the Central line)

A History of Capitalism
According to the Jubilee Line
by John O'Farrell
(the Jubilee line)

Musical Direction

Heads and Straights
by Lucy Wadham
(the Circle line)

Earthbound
by Paul Morley
(the Bakerloo line)

The Blue Riband
by Peter York
(the Piccadilly line)

Tube Knowledge

What We Talk About When We Talk About The Tube
by John Lanchester
(the District line)

A Good Parcel of English Soil
by Richard Mabey
(the Metropolitan line)

A Breath of Fresh Air

A Good Parcel of English Soil
by Richard Mabey
(the Metropolitan line)

Design for Life

Waterloo – City, City – Waterloo
by Leanne Shapton
(the Waterloo & City line)

Buttoned-Up
by Fantastic Man
(the East London line)

Drift
by Philippe Parreno
(the Hammersmith & City line)